Contents

Participation in Practice

CHILDREN AND YOUNG PEOPLE
AS PARTNERS IN CHANGE

Carolyne Willow

Foreword by Baroness Massey of Darwen
and Hilton Dawson, MP

The
Children's
Society

First published in 2002

The Children's Society
Edward Rudolf House
Margery Street
London WC1X 0JL

A catalogue record of this book is available from the British Library.

ISBN 1 899783 40 7

Acknowledgements

We are extremely grateful to all of the young people who helped make this book.

For help in the preparation of the case studies:
Aaron Bawden
Carlianne Fowler
Christopher Martin
Elaine Steed
Polly Matthews
Saidat Jimoh

Steering Group members:
James Anderson
Matthew Roberts
Tim Davies

Thanks also to the following for commenting on the draft manuscript: Dorothy Blatcher, Gerison Landsdown, Liam Cairns, Rachel Hodgkin and Richard Grant; and to Julie McLarnon, Simon Hepburn, Janet Wyllie, Jenny Frank, Maureen Murray and Mike Jones for all their help.

Finally, a huge thank you to Bill Badham who helped in so many ways.

Foreword

The active participation of children and young people can help to bring about real change in the world, partly because of the changes that it brings in ourselves.

Children and young people know more than we do about lots of things. They bring great ideas from a different perspective. Their interest, energy and commitment move things along.

They can challenge just by stating the obvious, they have tighter timescales with no reason to be patient with ours. They make all those meetings a great deal more fun.

The changes that we can make now by encouraging them to participate in the structures in society which affect all our lives will be nothing compared to successive generations of future citizens nurtured on good listening and respect accorded to them as children. The messages in this book encourage such an approach.

BARONESS MASSEY OF DARWEN
HILTON DAWSON, MP
Joint Chairs – All Party
Parliamentary Group for Children

Preface

As a young person I've seen that there are many times children and young people are not listened to when decisions are made that affect us. Yet under the United Nations Convention on the Rights of the Child, young people do have a right to be listened to. The importance of participation, however, is more than that. With rights come responsibilities; with the involvement of children and young people comes a sense of belonging, of ownership and of motivation. Participation is highly important to the ongoing success of any work with children and young people. Not only does it ensure that what is being provided is the right thing, but it also engages us, gets us involved and gives us responsibilities.

For every organisation there will be different challenges, pitfalls and, more importantly, benefits from the participation of children and young people. It is essential to strive to find the right formula and this is often a long process. This book aims to assist in making this happen. The time is not for talking but for doing.

TIM DAVIES
Steering Group member

Participation is like dancing the Macarena. Many love it – it's electric. But some hate it and don't like the group pressure. Others just feel a bit silly and self-conscious. Many of us need a bit of encouragement to get up and get started. Of course no one has to join in, but you may feel you ought to. Probably no one is judging anyone else, but you feel they might be. There is something to join in and others to join in with, but you can also do your own thing or sit and watch from the sides. Some come to it with a natural flair, others will need a bit more practice. Someone else may have put the music on, but you could always make other requests, or even take over the decks.

A book on participation needs a definition of participation. This one arose while watching 600 young carers dancing to the Macarena under the big top at the first annual young carers' festival at the YMCA at Fairthorne Manor in June 2000.

Creating opportunities for children and young people to participate in influencing decisions that affect them is not optional, it is essential. (We had, at least, to provide music at the festival!) The opportunity to participate genuinely in decision-making is a right, a civil right, a human right and a right of citizenship. It is set out in the United Nations Convention on the Rights of the Child of 1989, ratified by the UK Government in December 1991.

Local and national government in the UK is increasingly taking notice of the UN Convention and expecting its implementation through the active participation of its younger citizens. But while the case for *why* participation may have been won, we are often not sure about the *how*, especially how to ensure the systematic participation of children and young people, including those most often marginalised due to, for example, age, race and disability. In 1999 Professor Alan Prout summed it up:

> *When it comes to the representation or inclusion of children per se in wider decision-making... initiatives have remained local, scattered, ad hoc, fragile and experimental.*

In this book, Carolyne Willow sets out the context for children and young people's involvement as citizens now, and draws on six case studies from across work in The Children's Society to illustrate how it can and needs to be done. The concluding chapter evaluates the key messages and their wider application.

It is a main tenet of this book, and central to the values of The Children's Society, that the inclusion of children and young people and the full implementation of the United Nations Convention on the

Rights of the Child will only be advanced significantly when accompanied by wider structural and political change. The case studies, therefore, each seek to show how direct practice can influence the relevant systems impacting upon children and young people. These include early years practices, health, education, child protection, services for disabled children, regeneration and urban renewal.

Participation is the keystone of the arch that is the United Nations Convention on the Rights of the Child. It is unique and holds the whole structure together. Without it the framework falls. Without the active participation of children and young people in the promotion of all their rights to a good childhood, none will be achieved effectively. Through its 90 or so projects, The Children's Society acknowledges this by looking to work alongside children and young people in difficult circumstances to be a positive force for change and to champion with them their rights to a good childhood.

In The Children's Society, we also realise this means getting our own house in order. With children and young people at the forefront, we have embarked on a journey that is transforming the organisation. With participation embedded as a core principle, the Society is increasingly involving children and young people in its decision-making across functions and departments, including in the governance of the organisation. In August 2001, the first annual conference of children and young people across the Society was held at which they elected a 20-strong Advisory Group which has five places to attend the governing Council. We have learned that the biggest barriers needing to be broken down are often our own attitudes and power as adults. For true transformation to occur we have to stick with it, believe in the benefits to the children and young people, to all the staff and to the health and effectiveness of the organisation as a whole. It needs dedicated time and resources, corporate ownership and 'stickability'. These are the themes in these pages.

BILL BADHAM
Programme Manager
Children in Communities

Introduction

MOVING TOWARDS A RIGHTS FOCUS

At the end of the 1970s, young people in care in England produced a "charter of rights", with a demand for:

The right to be able to make our own decisions and to have real influence over those decisions we are sometimes considered too thick to participate in.[1]

Now, two and a half decades later, children and young people across the world have a comprehensive set of rights, including the right to have their views given due weight in all decisions that affect them. In December 1991 the UK Government formally ratified these rights. They are brought together in the UN Convention on the Rights of the Child (UNCRC) and apply to everyone from birth to 18 years.

In the ten years since the UK Government ratified the UNCRC, participatory initiatives and consultation projects have mushroomed within public bodies and children's charities. Everybody's talking about listening to and including children and young people in decision-making. Local authorities led the way from the late 1980s, appointing children's rights and advocacy officers, and setting up participation projects. Even the structures and culture of central government are now changing, with the establishment of young people's advisory fora and the publication of guidelines for Government departments for achieving effective participation with children and young people.[2]

A host of documents and publications have been published, aimed at developing policy and practice in line with the UNCRC. Checklists, toolkits, manuals, frameworks and standards have all been produced to address the organisational and cultural shift that needs to take place to precipitate effective participation in decision-making.

The Children's Society is one of many organisations whose approach to meeting children's and young people's needs has been transformed during the past decade. Central to this process has been the growing acknowledgement of the role of young citizens in proposing and effecting change – in their individual lives, in their environments and in wider society.

WHAT DOES PARTICIPATION MEAN?

Roger Hart[3] has described participation as:

The process of sharing decisions which affect one's life and the life of the community in which one lives. It is the means by which a democracy is built and it is a standard against which democracies should be measured. Participation is the fundamental right of citizenship.

From this perspective, participation is not simply about being listened to or being consulted – it also about influencing decision-making and achieving change.

The young people in care who developed the charter of rights were extremely clear-headed about the need for change. Unfortunately, those involved in many of the participatory projects and initiatives today do not always have such focus. We seem to have become very adept at listening to children's and young people's concerns and ideas, but not so skilled at involving them in proposing and implementing solutions.

Young people in the 1970s, as now, were not afraid of the language of rights. Fitting participation within a human rights framework helps to maintain the focus on entitlement and social justice. Rather than being seen as yet another thing adults do to children, from this perspective participatory activities are about supporting children and young people to challenge and change structures and systems that harm, exclude or ignore them. Without a human rights framework, adults can too easily slip into seeing participation as an end in itself.

Listening to and respecting children and young people can engage those previously deemed troublesome or marginalised, and it can enhance their relationships with adults. It can also offer them valuable opportunities to develop their social and communication skills, and to increase knowledge and learning. These are some of the positive outcomes and reasons for promoting participation. But these benefits will not lead to cultural or organisational change.

Further, focusing exclusively on the enormous benefits of promoting children's and young people's participation can sometimes obscure that being listened to and taken seriously is a fundamental human right:

> The benefits of participation are not only to society in general but more specifically to young people and to the organisations engaging them... However, participation should not be seen in a purely utilitarian light – that young people will get better jobs or service providers will do their jobs better. It must be seen as a fundamental right as expressed in Article 12 of the United Nations Convention on the Rights of the Child, and not something to be withdrawn if it fails to produce the right outputs.[4]

AIM, STRUCTURE AND CONTENTS OF THE BOOK

This publication aims to promote wider respect for children's and young people's participation rights, and a greater understanding of how they can be realised. It is aimed at supporting organisational change, but we hope it will also be of value to individual practitioners. In sharing some of the work of The Children's Society here, it is hoped that other organisations and individuals will be further inspired and motivated to join forces with children and young people to improve their lives and to enhance their status and position in society.

The book begins with the policy context for children's and young people's participation. This outlines emerging opportunities for young citizens to become involved in a range of decision-making processes. An exploration of the case for children's and young people's participation follows in Chapter 2, together with an analysis of some of the barriers to progress. The chapter ends with questions about who benefits from participation, and how receptive individuals and organisations are to children's and young people's ideas and proposals.

Six case studies are then included to show a selection of approaches taken by The Children's Society in supporting children and young people to influence decision-making in a number of settings, including in their schools, in child protection decisions, in their neighbourhoods, through their local authorities, and in national practice and policy developments. Each case study explores positive learning as well as tensions and difficulties.

The concluding chapter brings together the lessons from The Children's Society's work and offers suggestions on how organisations can show respect for children's and young people's participation rights in concrete, practical ways.

A personal action plan is included on pages 137–139 to encourage ongoing reflection and progress.

CHAPTER 1

Policy context for children's and young people's participation

EVERYBODY'S DOING IT: PROMOTING CHILDREN AND YOUNG PEOPLE'S PARTICIPATION

Legislation and government guidance increasingly encourage young citizens to take their place at decision-making tables. New groups and organisations have emerged – some run exclusively by young people – with the principal aim of promoting children's and young people's effective participation. The importance of listening to and engaging with children and young people has been stressed in major social policy programmes aimed at, for example, transforming local authority children's services, ending child poverty in a generation and reforming the NHS. Many children's charities have begun a period of transition, from being organisations working *for* or *on behalf of* children and young people, to organisations working *with* children and young people. There are even signs that central government is being modernised to make way for children and young people, following the launch of the Children's and Young People's Unit in England in November 2000.[1]

Listening to children and young people, and promoting their participation in a range of decision-making processes, is now valued and credible. Legislation has brought about change but the vision and political will of many politicians, especially at a local level, has also been enormously important. Adults have woken up to the fact that many of the social and political problems facing us in the birth of the new millennium require new ideas, approaches and solutions that can only emerge through positive dialogue and partnerships between young and old.

There are many participatory spaces where children and young people can claim their right to take part as members of their local communities, and society as a whole. Questions about why children and young people should be listened to and taken seriously are explored in Chapter 2. What follows here is background information on the UNCRC, and an overview of the range of opportunities to promote children's and young people's participation in decision-making:

* about their own lives;
* within their local neighbourhoods and communities;
* in national public policy-making.

A table on pages 21–27 summarises the major opportunities currently available to children and young people to take part in service and policy development at a local level.

A GLOBAL COMMITMENT TO HUMAN RIGHTS

It is now a decade since the UK Government pledged to make all laws, policies and practices fully compatible with the UNCRC.[2]

The Convention is a global statement of what children need to lead happy, fulfilling and healthy lives. It applies to all babies, children and young people from birth to 18 years. This international treaty, adopted by the United Nations on 20 November 1989, has been signed by all but two of the world's eligible countries.[3] It took ten years to develop after Poland made the initial proposal at the end of the International Year of the Child in 1979.

Although other human rights treaties apply to babies, children and young people,[4] the UNCRC ensures governments across the world recognise and meet children's particular needs.

The UNCRC underlines that children are especially vulnerable to mistreatment and exploitation. Working from a global perspective, it addresses the damaging effects on children of poverty, poor healthcare, wars and violence. It acknowledges the primary importance of play and learning, and gives special attention to children in precarious situations – such as those living away from home, refugee children and children involved in criminal justice systems. The UNCRC supports the role of parents in guiding children and young people, in line with their 'evolving capacities'. It also places a duty on governments to support parents, especially to promote non-violence within families.

The adoption of the UNCRC by the UN was a major breakthrough for children in three main respects. First, it signalled that the world's politicians were now committed to giving the young their fair share of attention and resources, enabling them to reach their fullest potential as human beings. Second, it granted children new rights to protection from all forms of violence and mistreatment in all settings, including in the family home. Third, it heralded the start of accepting and valuing all children as individuals worthy of fundamental civil rights, including: the right to express their views; the right to association and to information; and the right to freedom of thought, conscience and religion.

The UNCRC promotes children as whole human beings with their own rights and needs. Its full implementation will one day see children treated universally as individual people in their own right and no longer viewed as appendages of parents or simply the passive recipients of educational or other social programmes.

There are 54 Articles in the Convention: 40 of these ascribe direct rights to children, while the remainder refer to the duties of governments to monitor, implement and report on progress.

ARTICLE 12

Article 12 of the UNCRC is perhaps most widely known, especially among children's charities, and groups and organisations run by young people. This key Article grants all children and young people who are able to form views the right to express and have their views taken into account in all matters that affect them. It also entitles children's and young people's views to be heard, directly or through a representative, in all judicial and administrative proceedings:

1. States Parties shall assure to the child who is capable of forming his or her own views the right to express those views freely in all matters affecting the child, the views of the child being given due weight in accordance with the age and maturity of the child.

2. For this purpose the child shall in particular be provided the opportunity to be heard in any judicial and administrative proceedings affecting the child, either directly, or through a representative or an appropriate body, in a manner consistent with the procedural rules of national law.

**Article 12 of the UN Convention
on the Rights of the Child**

In 1996, a UK-wide children's rights organisation run entirely by under-18-year-olds was launched, called Article 12. The activities of this organisation have undoubtedly helped to raise the profile of children's right to participate in decision-making. With funding from the Department of Health, the group is currently preparing a Children's Rights Information Pack for under-18-year-olds, which will include a promotional video on the UNCRC.

ARTICLE 23

Article 23 of the UNCRC gives young disabled people important rights to participate actively in their communities. While all the rights in the UNCRC, including Article 12, apply equally to young disabled people, the existence of Article 23 reminds governments and other public bodies of their duty to tackle the continuing social exclusion and discrimination faced by young disabled people:

1. States Parties recognise that a mentally or physically disabled child should enjoy a full and decent life, in conditions which ensure dignity, promote self-reliance, and facilitate the child's active participation in the community...

3. Recognising the special needs of a disabled child, assistance... [shall be] in a manner conducive to the child's achieving the fullest possible social integration and individual development, including his or her cultural and spiritual development.

**Extracts from Article 23 of the UN Convention
on the Rights of the Child**

ARTICLE 13

The right to freedom of expression, as prescribed by Article 13 of the UNCRC, is also pertinent to promoting children's effective participation. This Article grants children the right to seek, receive and disseminate all kinds of information and ideas in a variety of forms:

1. The child shall have the right to freedom of expression: this right shall include the freedom to seek, receive and impart information and ideas of all kinds, regardless of frontiers, either orally, in writing or in print, in the form of art, or through any other media of the child's choice.

2. The exercise of this right may be subject to certain restrictions, but these shall only be such as are provided by law and are necessary:
(a) For the respect of the rights or reputations of others; or
(b) For the protection of national security or of public order (ordre public) or of public health or morals.

Article 13 of the UN Convention
on the Rights of the Child

Children have no legal means of individually or collectively challenging breaches of their Convention rights. They cannot use domestic or international courts to remedy violations. This, however, does not mean the Convention has no bite.

DUTIES OF RATIFICATION

When governments ratify the UNCRC, they have a duty to report on progress to the Committee on the Rights of the Child, initially after two years and every five years thereafter. Committee members are international adult experts on children's rights, nominated by UN member states. They meet in Geneva three times a year to consider critically progress reports submitted by governments. Importantly, they also consider reports and submissions from non-governmental organisations, including those prepared by children and young people. At the end of the 1990s, three separate consultations with over 1,000 children and young people were carried out across the UK to ascertain how well the UNCRC is being respected.[5] These reports have been submitted to the Committee on the Rights of the Child for when it examines the UK Government's report in September 2002.[6]

The UNCRC is now increasingly cited in judicial and administrative proceedings concerning children. The European Court of Human Rights has, for example, referred to it in recent judgements about UK law and practice. Social workers, doctors, playworkers and other professionals working with children are slowly becoming more aware of its provisions, and using it to promote children's participation in decision-making. Over 400 statutory and voluntary bodies[7] have formally adopted it: some local authorities have displayed exceptional commitment to children's rights by using the UNCRC as the planning framework for all their children's services.[8] Finally, the UNCRC has turned into an important lobbying tool for groups and organisations run by young people, with Article 12 taking prominence as children and young people increasingly claim their right to be listened to and taken seriously.

BRINGING RIGHTS HOME: THE HUMAN RIGHTS ACT 1998

On 2 October 2000, the Human Rights Act 1998 came into force across the UK, having already been in operation in Scotland since 1999. The Home Secretary at the time, Jack Straw, described this process of incorporating the European Convention on Human Rights into domestic law as "bringing rights home".

The Human Rights Act 1998 grants all UK citizens, including children, all the rights contained in the European Convention. The Act allows challenges to UK laws to be made in domestic courts, whereas before they could only be settled in the European Court of Human Rights in Strasbourg. Crucially, it also requires all new laws to be compatible with the rights contained in the European Convention on Human Rights.

The European Convention on Human Rights was prepared after the atrocities of the Second World War, and gives particular attention to the preservation of individual freedoms. For example, citizens are granted the right to a fair trial, to respect for private and family life, and to protection from inhuman or degrading treatment or punishment. Other civil liberties, such as freedom of expression and the right to free assembly and association, are also covered, as is freedom of thought, conscience and religion.

A LACK OF FOCUS ON CHILDREN AND YOUNG PEOPLE

There is one right in the European Convention that arguably applies more to under-18-year-olds:

No person shall be denied the right to education.

Extract from Article 2 of the First Protocol of the European Convention on Human Rights

However, the Article continues to explain that governments must:

... respect the right of parents to ensure such education and teaching is in conformity with their own religious and philosophical convictions.

The European Convention on Human Rights is not tailored to meet the breadth of children's experiences and needs. For example, there is no mention of the particular needs of children and young people involved in criminal justice systems. Further, Article 6, the right to a fair trial, has so far not been applied to educational administrative procedures such as school admission or exclusion processes.

Despite its limitations, the European Convention has been used positively to force changes in UK law and policy, for example, relating to corporal punishment in schools, access to social services files, and criminal proceedings for child defendants. There is hope that, coupled with the provisions of the UNCRC, the Human Rights Act 1998 will at least be used to remedy some of the most severe breaches of children's human rights. These include: the degrading treatment of young asylum-seekers and refugees; the widespread parental physical punishment of babies and children; and the increasing number of young people being locked up in institutions, which were described by the Chief Inspector of Prisons in 1997 as "unacceptable in a civilised society" and "institutionalised child abuse".[9] It is also likely that the extension of child curfew schemes to under-16s will, if implemented by local authorities and the police, lead to test cases under Article 8 of the European Convention; the right to respect for private and family life.[10]

CHILDREN TAKING PART IN DECISIONS ABOUT THEIR OWN LIVES

FAMILY LIFE

While children and young people in or leaving care have legal rights to participate in decisions about their lives, children in families have no such entitlements.[11] Parents in England and Wales do not have a legal responsibility to consult children about important decisions that affect them, such as moving house, taking in a lodger, changing employment or deciding to foster or adopt a child.

Even when decisions can have grave consequences for children, such as when parents separate, they have no automatic right to be consulted and do not even get the chance to voice their wishes through the court process if their parents opt for an 'amicable split'. When parental conflict arises about children, there is no guarantee that children will be represented separately in court proceedings. A court welfare officer may be appointed but their role is to represent their professional judgement of what is in the child's best interests. This can be very different from articulating the child's wishes and feelings, or helping the child to express their views and concerns directly.[12] Children can be represented separately by guardians *ad litem* or lawyers but this does not happen consistently. Indeed, a proposal aimed at ensuring that all children involved in private family law proceedings be offered separate representation in the new Children and Family Court Advisory and Support Service (CAFCASS) was rejected on the grounds of cost.

The Committee on the Rights of the Child (the international monitoring body for the UNCRC) recommends that governments define parental responsibilities in law.[13] This has not happened in England and Wales but the Children (Scotland) Act 1995 does outline the responsibilities of parents, including the requirement to "have regard as far as is practicable" to the views of children and young people whenever they are making "major decisions". Parents are expected to take into account children's age and maturity, although there is a legal presumption that over-12-year-olds are "of sufficient age and maturity to form a view". Other countries, such as Finland, Norway and Sweden, require parents to respect children and to have regard to their growing independence. Finland's Child Custody and Right of Access Act 1983, for example, states that:

> *A child shall be brought up in the spirit of understanding, security and love. He shall not be subdued, corporally punished or otherwise humiliated. His growth towards independence, responsibility and adulthood shall be encouraged, supported and assisted.*[14]

EDUCATION

Most children in the UK spend 11 years in formal education. Now that school gates have been opened to three- and four-year-olds[15] and more young people are encouraged to stay on, this period of time can stretch to 15 years. Yet children and young people have limited rights to be consulted about decisions affecting their education. The exception is in the area of special educational needs, where children's role in assessment is formally acknowledged. The Code of Practice on the Identification and Assessment of Special Educational Needs, which came into force in September 1994, promotes children's and young people's participation in the assessment process. A revised code came into effect in January 2002, and is even more explicit about the need to include children and young people in their individual assessments and in the wider school decision-making:[16]

> *Pastoral programmes should ensure that all pupils are involved in and can contribute to both their own education and the wider life of the school... All schools should ensure that pupils with special educational needs are fully involved in all aspects of the life of the school and are enabled to have an equal voice.*

There is also a requirement to involve looked-after children and young people in the development of their personal education plans, which local authorities are required to prepare within 20 school days of them entering care.[17]

In September 2001 the Government published a White Paper – Schools: Achieving Success – that included a promise to increase student participation:

> *We will encourage schools to help to develop rounded individuals,*

by supporting young people's participation in decisions affecting them, introducing citizenship into the curriculum and extending opportunities to participate in out-of-school activities.

A consultation document from OFSTED[18] proposed to pilot the use of surveys to gather the views and ideas of secondary school students during inspections. The document also includes a commitment to consider how best to include younger children in the inspection process.

On the whole, however, education procedures suggest accountability to the parents and carers rather than to the student. Too often, education continues to be perceived as a service for parents and carers, rather than as a process through which individual children and young people can develop their fullest potential as human beings.[19] For example, Home-School Agreements, introduced in September 1999, are expressly aimed at increasing the involvement of parents in their children's education. They include information on the quality of teaching and the school's ethos, discipline and homework. Although school students can be asked to sign the Agreements, they have no legal right to be consulted when they are being drafted.

Section 39 of the School Standards and Framework Act 1998 requires governing bodies to establish and publicise complaints procedures, but students have no right to independent advocacy, and, unlike social services complaints procedures, there is no requirement for an "independent person" to be involved in the process. There is still a presumption that parents will complain, not children, and high-profile cases show that schools and local education authorities are often inflexible to children's basic wishes. For instance, in February 2000, a teenager from the North-East won the right to wear trousers at school, following intervention from the Equal Opportunities Commission. The girl's mother had spent almost three years, on her daughter's behalf, trying to persuade her daughter's headteacher and her local education authority that allowing girls to wear trousers would not lead to a breakdown in discipline, as they claimed.

The Special Educational Needs and Disability Act 2001 grants young disabled people new rights to attend mainstream schools.

However, parents of young disabled people will be able to veto inclusive education, irrespective of the views of their children.[20] The Act also extends the provisions of the Disability Discrimination Act 1995 to cover schools and other educational settings.

HEALTH AND SOCIAL SERVICES

Since the Gillick case was resolved in 1986, the principle of children's "evolving capacities" has been enshrined in UK law. Victoria Gillick, a Roman Catholic mother of ten children, took her health authority to court to prohibit her daughters from being able to consent to contraceptive advice or treatment. The case reached the House of Lords where the majority decision was that under-16-year-olds can give consent to medical treatment. Lord Scarman, one of the law lords deciding the case, placed great emphasis on an earlier judgement by Lord Denning who referred to parents' "dwindling right... [which starts with] control and ends with little more than advice". As a result, there is no fixed age in law for under-16s to consent to medical advice or treatment, or to play a direct role in civil proceedings such as divorce or adoption hearings. Instead, they have to show they are competent, and understand both the proceedings and the implications of their wishes.

Questions about whether individual children and young people are 'Gillick competent' are now routinely made in civil proceedings and health settings, where judges and doctors exercise enormous discretion. There have been some very disappointing judgements: for example, in 1991 a young woman, two months from her 16th birthday, was deemed not to be Gillick competent because she refused to consent to psychiatric drugs. While the Gillick case was a great step forward for children's human rights, there is still a long way to go before adults dispense with preconceived ideas and prejudices before assessing children's competencies. A competent child is often in the eye of the beholder.

THE CHILDREN ACT 1989

Children's right to be listened to and taken seriously was given a new lease of life when the Children Act 1989 came into force in October 1991. Although local authorities in England and Wales have had a duty to ascertain the wishes and feelings of children in their care since 1975,[21] the Children Act 1989 is often credited with single-handedly promoting the participation rights of children in care.

Section 22(4) of the Children Act states that before local authorities make any decisions about a child in their care, or who they are proposing to look after, they should:

> ... *so far as is reasonably practicable, ascertain the wishes and feelings of the child... regarding the matter to be decided.*

Section 22(5) further states that local authorities should give "due consideration" to children's wishes and feelings, according to their age and understanding, and that they should also take into account children's "religious persuasion, racial origin and cultural and linguistic background". A raft of secondary legislation, guidance, research, national standards[22] and high-profile programmes to improve the care system's effectiveness has reinforced these requirements. There have been positive reports of local authorities properly consulting and involving children in planning their care.[23] Yet still children and young people complain that social services are not listening to them, or taking them seriously.

The Government's own evaluation of local authorities' performance in this area during 1999–2000 concluded that:

> ... *children and young people's participation remains a key area for development for many councils. There was good evidence... of progress in involving children in the planning and delivery of services, although in many cases developments were patchy and needed to be part of an integrated strategy. However, many fewer councils were performing well in terms of involving individual children in decisions about their own care.*[24]

Although most participation rights in the Children Act 1989 relate to the care system, the Act also supports the Gillick principle by permitting children involved in child protection procedures to refuse consent to medical and psychiatric examinations if they are deemed to have sufficient understanding. Children and young people with sufficient understanding are also given the right to apply to courts for orders relating to who they live with, for example, and contact with parents or other relatives. However, a judge must first be satisfied that the child or young person understands the processes and possible implications. This has led to inconsistent practice.

TAKING PART IN DECISIONS IN NEIGHBOURHOODS AND COMMUNITIES

The 1990s brought major opportunities for citizen participation. Local authorities have been at the hub of an array of initiatives set up, for example, to protect the environment; to rebuild communities and tackle social exclusion; and to modernise local government and improve the effectiveness of services. The involvement of local people has been central to these developments.

In addition, citizen participation has been promoted within specific services such as in health and social care, youth work and juvenile justice. All these initiatives are summarised in the table on pages 21–27. What follows is a brief outline of the role of children and young people in broad government programmes to protect the environment, tackle social exclusion and to improve local democracy.

PROTECTING THE ENVIRONMENT

Following the first Earth Summit in Rio in 1992, local authorities across England and Wales, together with their global counterparts, have actively pursued policies and activities that help to protect the environment and meet the challenges of the 21st century. This international programme – called Agenda 21 – places emphasis on young people's participation in sustainable development:

> *The creativity, ideals and courage of the youth of the world should be mobilized to forge a global partnership in order to achieve sustainable development and ensure a better future for all.*
>
> *Principle 21 of the Rio Declaration on Environment and Development, June 1992*

By the time of the Earth Summit II, held in New York in 1997, 90 per cent of UK local authorities had "some form of local Agenda 21 process".[25] Young people have been active participants in many initiatives, carrying out a broad range of activities from recycling campaigns, to transport and pollution surveys to public education and consultation.[26] Sustainable development is now included in the Best Value process, which also underlines the importance of public involvement in service review and development.

REBUILDING COMMUNITIES AND TACKLING SOCIAL EXCLUSION

The primary focus for local communities in need of financial and social investment has, in recent years, been the Single Regeneration Budget (SRB). Launched in 1994, its purpose is to support regeneration initiatives carried out by local partnerships across England. One of the objectives of the SRB is to "address social exclusion and improving opportunities for the disadvantaged". Successful bids for the sixth and final round were announced in August 2000. Out of 143 approved schemes, 41 referred to outcomes for children and young people but only three were exclusively targeted at increasing children's and young people's participation in their communities.

The Government's New Deal for Communities programme (NDC), set up in 1998, presents a further opportunity for young people to work in partnership with other local stakeholders to improve their communities. This ten-year initiative aims to support the most deprived communities in England by: tackling unemployment; improving health; reducing crime; and raising educational achievement. NDC is an experimental programme and, as such, there will not be any further rounds of NDC.

In July 2000, the Government announced the new Children's Fund, worth £450 million across three years, the aim of which was:

> ... to prevent children falling into drug abuse, truancy, exclusion, unemployment and crime, as well as raising aspirations and preventing underachievement.

The cross-government Children and Young People's Unit manages this England-wide Fund.[27] Its resources are divided into two major activities: preventing child poverty and disadvantage through local services; and helping children to reach their full potential through supporting local community and voluntary groups. The promotional information for the Fund has positively stressed the importance of children's and young people's participation.

In Wales, the Communities First programme has invested £83 million between 2001 and 2003 in 100 communities experiencing high levels of poverty and social exclusion. The programme demands that children and young people are consulted and included in the development of local initiatives and that their views and ideas are acted on.[28]

IMPROVING LOCAL DEMOCRACY AND THE EFFECTIVENESS OF SERVICES

Just over a year after taking office, the new Labour Government published a White Paper[29] on modernising local government, stressing the need for improved local democracy:

The Government wishes to see consultation and participation embedded into the culture of all councils, including parishes, and undertaken across a wide range of each council's responsibilities.

The White Paper was followed by the Local Government Act 2000. Section 4, which came into effect at the end of September 2000, requires all local authorities to prepare a community strategy:

... for promoting or improving the economic, social and environmental wellbeing of their area and contributing to the achievement of sustainable development in the United Kingdom.

Further, local authorities "must consult and seek the participation of such persons as they consider appropriate" when preparing these strategies.

Prior to the above developments, the Local Government Act 1999 introduced a new requirement for local authorities to carry out Best Value reviews of all their services, using the 'four Cs' – challenge, consult, compare and compete. All councils are required to carry out three-yearly 'user satisfaction surveys' as well as prepare annual Performance Plans that incorporate the wishes and priorities of local people, including children and young people. Performance indicators for 2001/2002 were published in December 2000.[30] However, although issues of gender, disability and race equality are incorporated into the corporate measures, no reference is made to the specific needs of young citizens.

Children's Services Planning Guidance, issued in 1996,[31] and currently being revised, stresses the need for consultation with children and young people:

It is important to remember that children and young people are users or potential users of the services, and their views should be sought and given due weight alongside those of parents and carers.

The user is a partner in the process rather than a passive recipient; effective consultation should be encouraged and contributions treated seriously and feedback given.

At the end of 2000, the Welsh Assembly published draft guidance for local authorities on strategic partnerships. The document stresses the absolute necessity of working in partnership with children and young people:[32]

In submitting their local strategies, authorities will be expected to have shown that children and young people across the whole spectrum, from all communities and backgrounds, have been involved in their production, and in what way.

Local Strategic Partnerships in England also present opportunities for children and young people to influence developments in their local environments. However, the strategic function of these partnerships and the difficulties many adults in the statutory and voluntary sectors have of working together effectively, diminish the chances of young citizens joining.

Service-specific initiatives probably have more appeal to children and young people, providing a range of opportunities for them to be involved in appraising and developing services.

Table 1 on pages 21–27 identifies service-specific initiatives that, together with the programmes outlined above, encourage children and young people to take part in service and policy development at a local level. As can be seen, Government guidance requires the involvement of children and young people in most cases, and sometimes legislation requires it. On other occasions, notably in the formal education system, the right of children and young people to participate in decision-making is hardly promoted at all.

Table 1 Article 12 in Action: Opportunities for children and young people to influence decision-making at a local level (according to policy areas).

The initiatives cover England and Wales, unless otherwise identified. In Wales, all children's services must take account of 'Children and Young People: a Framework for Partnership', which demands the full involvement of children and young people in the planning and delivery of services that affect them.

Type of initiative	Target group	Opportunities to participate
PROTECTING THE ENVIRONMENT		
Local Agenda 21	All children and young people	In July 2000 the Department for the Environment, Transport and the Regions (DETR) published a handbook on sustainable development, *Local Quality of Life Counts*. This builds on positive practice at a local level and gives 29 indicators for measuring progress. Indicator 21 promotes social participation; indicator 23 community involvement; and indicator 24 tenant satisfaction and participation.
TACKLING SOCIAL EXCLUSION AND NEIGHBOURHOOD RENEWAL		
Single Regeneration Budget (SRB), England	All children and young people in deprived areas	Launched in 1994, the SRB seeks to develop local regeneration. Its objectives include improving the educational opportunities of local people; tackling social exclusion and disadvantage; and reducing crime and drug abuse and promoting community safety. DETR Round 6 Bidding Guidance (1999) stressed the need to "engage the talents and resources of the whole community" in local initiatives.

Type of initiative	Target group	Opportunities to participate
National Strategy for Neighbourhood Renewal	All children and young people in deprived communities	In England, the Government's three-year action plan on neighbourhood renewal (January 2001) introduced a new "Community Empowerment Fund" for community and voluntary sector participation, and "Community Chests" to support self-help and mutual aid. Together they are worth at least £86 million.
New Deal for Communities, England	All children and young people in 34 deprived communities	Launched in 1998, this programme gives deprived communities of between one and four thousand households "intensive and co-ordinated support". Active community involvement is seen as essential to the success of local partnerships.
Communities First, Wales	All children and young people in 100 deprived communities	Communities First represents £83m over three years to 100 communities. It requires the involvement of children and young people from all backgrounds and cultures in developing plans that will be delivered through multi-agency partnerships.
Children's Fund, England	Children and young people at risk of social exclusion, or living in poverty	Children's and young people's active involvement is a key feature of the Children's Fund, which was launched in England in 2001. It allocates £450 million across three years to preventive services and to local community groups, including those led by children and young people. Partnerships are expected to take the views of young people on board, and involve them in the design and delivery of services. The Children's Fund Local Network, administered by the Community Foundation Network, encourages the setting up of projects "that give children and young people the chance to express their opinions and give advice on matters that concern them".

Type of initiative	Target group	Opportunities to participate
LOCAL DEMOCRACY		
Best Value Reviews	All children and young people	All councils are required to carry out three-yearly 'user satisfaction surveys' as well as prepare annual Performance Plans that incorporate the wishes and priorities of local people, including children and young people. The Performance Indicators for 2001/2002 refer to gender, disability and race equality, but there is no mention of the specific needs of young citizens.
Community Strategies	All children and young people	Part 1 of the Local Government Act 2000 requires local authorities to promote the economic, social and environmental wellbeing of local areas. Part 4 of the Act, which came into effect in September 2000, requires local authorities to develop community strategies with local people and partner organisations.
EARLY YEARS		
Early Years Development and Childcare Plans	All children from birth to 14 years; up to 16 years for young disabled people and those with special educational needs	Since 1999 local authorities and other providers have developed Plans to "enhance the care, play and educational experience of young children" and improve the care and play experiences of children into their teenage years. Planning guidance[33] from the DfEE requires consultation with children.
Sure Start	Under-four-year-olds	There is no requirement to consult young children about local Sure Start programmes. However, it is now accepted good practice that young service users should be included in decision-making wherever possible, and in ways suitable to their age and understanding. Young parents (under-18-year-olds) can be members of local programme boards; they should be consulted when local programmes are being developed; and they should be involved in the running and evaluation of services.

Type of initiative	Target group	Opportunities to participate
EDUCATION		
Behaviour Support Plans	All children and young people of school age	Local education authorities are required to consult parent representatives when they prepare these Plans. The Plans cover support to schools, including training and guidance, as well as support to individual children, young people and their parents or carers.
Charter Mark Award for Schools	All school students	Criterion 4 of the Charter Mark Guide for Schools stresses the need to promote customer choice and information. There is an expectation that the wishes of parents and children and young people are reflected in local school development plans, and that the needs of young disabled people are taken into account in school planning and service provision.
National Healthy School Standard	All school students	The Healthy School Standard is part of the larger Healthy Schools programme led by the Department for Education and Skills and the Department of Health. A key aspect of the Standard is "giving pupils a voice", which incorporates curriculum planning and policy development.
Education Action Zones, England	All children and young people of school age in a particular locality	These are local partnerships set up to raise educational standards in disadvantaged urban and rural areas across England. Parental involvement is seen to be central to the success of the Zones and some are establishing Pupil Councils to enable active pupil engagement in real issues.
Education Development Plans	All children and young people of school age	Local education authorities are only required to consult governing bodies and headteachers when preparing these three-year strategic Plans.

Type of initiative	Target group	Opportunities to participate
Education Development Plans *continued*		DfEE guidance omits to describe the role of children and young people in developing these important Plans. The 1998 guidance suggested a long list of consultees, including parents and representatives of local religious, community, business and voluntary organisations but children and young people were noticeably absent.
YOUTH SUPPORT		
Connexions Partnerships, England	13- to 19-year-olds for non-disabled young people; up to 25 years if disabled	Connexions is currently being piloted in 16 areas across England. The service will be delivered through "Personal Advisers", who will advise, guide and support young people, "preparing them to be citizens, potential parents and productive, fulfilled members of their local community." Young people's active involvement in the design and governance of local Connexions services is positively promoted.[34]
Children and Youth Partnership Fund, Wales	8- to 13-year-olds	The Children and Youth Partnership Fund aims "to promote local initiatives to lift young people's educational achievements, improve health and encourage them to partake in creative activities in their communities to lead them away from crime, drugs and truancy".
HEALTH AND SOCIAL CARE		
Health Act 1999, England	All children and young people	Section 31 of the Health Act 1999 allows health authorities, NHS trusts, primary care trusts and local authorities to pool funds to improve services for users. There is an expectation that statutory agencies will work closely with users and the wider community in identifying unmet need and ways of improving services.

Type of initiative	Target group	Opportunities to participate
Health Act 1999, England *continued*		In Wales, distinctive legislation is emerging to abolish Health Authorities and develop Local Health Boards that must meet with the expectations of *Children and Young People: a Framework for Partnership*.
Health Action Zones, England	All children and young people in a particular locality	Since April 1998, 26 Zones have been established to tackle health inequality and to modernise services. Two of seven underpinning principles stress the need to consult and involve members of the public.
Quality Protects programme, England and Children First, Wales	Children and young people in contact with social services, especially those in public care	Children's and young people's participation is central to this five-year Quality Protects programme. Objective 8 expects local authorities to involve and consult children and young people in the development of services. Local councils are also advised to develop independent advocacy services to ensure children and young people's views are taken seriously. The Quality Protects programme has established a national young people's reference group to ensure the views of young people are fully incorporated into the programme. Objective 9 of the Children First programme in Wales promotes "the need to involve actively users and carers in planning services and tailoring individual packages of care". Children's Rights Officers and Advocates (CROA) has produced a national training pack called *Total Respect* on looked-after children's and young people's participation for the Department of Health.[35]

Type of initiative	Target group	Opportunities to participate
YOUTH JUSTICE AND CRIME PREVENTION		
Youth Justice Plans	All children and young people, especially those involved in crime	These Plans are to be prepared annually by all local agencies working with children and young people involved in crime. The Plans should be based on local crime audits (see Crime and Disorder Partnerships, page 27).
Crime and Disorder Partnerships	All children and young people	The Crime and Disorder Act 1998 builds on existing duties of police authorities to consult and involve the public, including children and young people, in crime prevention. Partnerships must carry out local crime audits and develop strategies for reducing crime and disorder. The Local Government Information Unit, in partnership with NACRO (National Association for the Care and Resettlement of Offenders), has produced guidance to ensure that young people are fully involved in promoting community safety.[36]

INFLUENCING NATIONAL PUBLIC POLICY

Children and young people have no vote. The law was last reformed in 1969, when the voting age was reduced from 21 to 18 years. The Children's Rights Alliance for England, in partnership with several young people's organisations, is lobbying for change, arguing that the continued exclusion of young people from the political process is illogical and unjust.[37]

Despite children's and young people's non-participation in the electoral process, there are a number of developments that underline their contribution to national policy- and decision-making.

VOICES FROM WITHIN

Following the joint Home Office and National Youth Agency *Listen Up* consultation with 500 13- to 25-year-olds in England during 1998–99, the Government appointed Paul Boateng as Minister for Young People in the summer of 2000.[38] Working directly with the Children and Young People's Unit, the Minister promised to include children and young people in all aspects of the Unit's work to combat child poverty and disadvantage. In 2001 the Unit launched its Core Principles and overarching strategy for children and young people. These will impact across Government departments, promoting children's and young people's active role in decision-making.[39]

The Department of Health's Quality Protects programme in England provides the best example within government of children and young people being engaged in national policy and service development. As the case study Ask Us! Young disabled people get active shows, over 200 young disabled people have been consulted about how Quality Protects can improve their lives. In addition, a series of roadshows were held during 2000 to obtain children's and young people's experiences and views of care, and a national young people's reference group has been formed to advise on children's and young people's participation across the whole Quality Protects programme.

There are other positive illustrations of the Department of Health's commitment to children's and young people's participation:

- The Children's National Service Framework,[40] currently being developed, stresses the need to consult and involve children and young people in decision-making.
- The organisation for young people in and leaving care in England, A National Voice, was commissioned to consult young people about leaving care reforms.
- The Social Services Inspectorate has employed young people with care experience as consultants and inspectors.
- The Department of Health has funded Article 12, an organisation run entirely by under-18-year-olds, to prepare a Children's Rights Information Pack (see page 8).

Other Government departments have initiated or supported national projects. For example, in 1998, the Department for the Environment, Transport and the Regions and the Department for Education and Employment held a Children's Parliament to enable children to share their ideas and views on protecting the environment. In May the following year, children took part in a Select Committee-style question and answer session with the Deputy Prime Minister, John Prescott, and the then Education Minister, Charles Clarke. A video was produced from the event, which attracted 10- and 11-year-olds from across England.

In November 1999 the Foreign and Commonwealth Office and Save the Children UK held a Children's Select Committee, involving 16 young people aged between 12 and 19 years. One of four key issues discussed was children's participation rights.[41] The Department for Education and Skills has supported the UK Youth Parliament (UKYP), which seeks to represent the concerns and views of 11- to 18-year-olds at a national level.[42] And two young people are to be part of the UK Government's delegation to the United Nations Special Session on Children, due to be held in New York in May 2002.[43]

Across Wales, there are positive developments not only to enhance children's and young people's participation at a local level but also nationally. In July 2001, the National Assembly for Wales issued a consultation paper called *Moving Forward: Listening to Children and Young People in Wales*, which included a proposal for a General Council with representatives from local children and young people's fora, and national and local groups.[44]

KNOCKING ON THE DOOR

The 1990s saw the birth of several new organisations led by children and young people, whose aim is to further the participation of children in decision-making at all levels of society. There are now organisations representing the rights and interests of young people in care in England, Northern Ireland, Scotland and Wales. Article 12 organisations exist in England and in Scotland, and groups have been formed to campaign for the rights of young disabled people. The Participation Education Group, initially based in the North East of England but now extending across the UK, has carried out a range of work to promote children's and young people's involvement in decision-making.[45] The UK Youth Parliament had its first national meeting in February 2001, and the National Black Youth Forum was launched in 2000 with the publication of its charter for black young people. During the run up to the 2001 general election, a consortium of young people-led organisations, including Article 12, the British Youth Council and the National Black Youth Forum, joined forces to campaign for the lowering of the voting age to 16 years.[46]

As well as organisations or groups run by children and young people themselves, several of the major children's charities have invested considerable time and resources in supporting children and young people to influence national decision-making processes. For instance, they have:

- carried out consultations on Government proposals;
- published materials prepared by children and young people about their experiences;
- arranged meetings between Government ministers and young people;
- provided funding and donated office space, meeting facilities and equipment;
- delivered training to children and young people on how to work with the media.

Listening to children and young people, and promoting their participation in a range of decision-making processes, is now a common aspiration among public services and in wider government structures and programmes. This chapter has shown that the contribution of young citizens is increasingly being recognised and supported. Debates have, on the whole, shifted from *why* adults should listen to *how* children's and young people's participation can be achieved. This is progress. However, the growing hunger among those working with children and young people for practical tips and signposts can sometimes conceal fundamental questions about the purpose of promoting participation, and the need for adults to change and to share power and decision-making. The next chapter critically examines developments in participation. It argues that real progress depends upon an understanding of children's and young people's social status and wider position in society, and a commitment to work with them to claim their human rights.

CHAPTER 2

Children's human rights and social inclusion

WHAT ARE WE DOING?

Listening, participation, empowerment, user involvement, consultation and inclusion: the buzz words of the new century. But what do they mean?

The main body of this chapter is an exploration of four inter-dependent themes concerning children's and young people's participation. These are:

- the case for including children and young people in all aspects of decision-making;
- how did we get here? An analysis of why children are excluded;
- breaking down the victim mentality: how adults can respect children;
- get involved for a change: acting on children's and young people's ideas and views.

A summary of guiding principles and recommendations for achieving change with children and young people is included in the concluding sections of this chapter.

There are several reasons why children and young people should be involved in all aspects of decision-making processes. These can be divided into three sub-headings: legal, political and social.

LEGAL CASE FOR CHILDREN'S AND YOUNG PEOPLE'S PARTICIPATION

The legal reasons for promoting children's and young people's participation largely rest on the provisions of the UNCRC (see pages 152–156), which has the status of international law. The UNCRC grants under-18-year-olds important participation rights, including: the right to have their views taken into account; the right to freedom of expression, thought, conscience and religion; freedom to meet and form associations with others; and the right to information. Young disabled people are granted additional rights to full integration and active participation in their communities.

No minimum age is given for participation in decision-making. Instead, Article 12 of the UNCRC states that any child who is capable of forming views has the right to have these views given "due weight" in all matters that affect them. Article 13 grants children the right to express their ideas and information in different ways – a reminder that human communication takes many forms and is not confined to language alone.

THE RIGHT TO FREEDOM OF EXPRESSION

Expressing views is not the exclusive pastime of teenagers or young adults. Babies and young children constantly communicate their individual wishes and feelings, starting with basic preferences but quickly developing more complex thoughts about what they enjoy doing, who they want to be with, and where they want to be:

> Besides looking outwards and reacting to people and things around them well before it used to be thought possible, babies express their views strongly and clearly through sounds and gestures, and in play when they make choices and show intense concentration and enjoyment... As infants start to use words, they make their views and wishes still more clearly known, unless they are strongly discouraged from doing so. The right to express a view and to be responded to begins to be honoured or withheld from birth and is soon expressed through sophisticated activities.[1]

There is another important provision in Article 12: that children should be able to express their views freely. Adults frequently thwart children's and young people's self-expression, sometimes without even knowing it. Young people's views and ideas are often met with destructive criticism, mockery, or, worse still, a patronising smile and silence. Children and young people usually have no problem accepting constructive criticism – it at least shows that their views are being taken seriously – but being patronised makes them feel insignificant and ignored as people.

Even when adults do try to take children and young people seriously, it is not uncommon for children to have to explain their ideas in a dialogue that would be seen as harassment or bullying if it occurred between two adults. An adult repeatedly questioning a child or young person can have the effect of silencing them:

> And sometimes when you ask adults for something they'll ask you all these questions and they know you're stuck and you can't say anything until you just give up.[2]

It often seems that for children's and young people's ideas to have currency, they must be articulated in ways that are far more sophisticated than adults', or their arguments must be extremely compelling and clever. Yet the UNCRC gives children and young people the right to express themselves in all kinds of ways. The challenge for adults is to respect, encourage and try to understand children's and young people's views and ideas. The diverse ways in which children and young people can communicate their ideas and wishes should be celebrated, not ridiculed or discouraged.

But the challenge is not just about enabling children and young people to communicate. Adults also need to develop positive and appropriate ways of expressing their ideas and views to children and young people. There is a risk that adults 'talk down' to children and young people, or that they use words that exclude them. The trick is to try to gauge what will work best for the children and young people involved, without trying to pass oneself off as a young person in the process. Adults who try to behave as if they were teenagers consistently do not engage children and young people.[3]

THE IMPORTANCE OF ADVOCACY

Independent advocacy – information, advice and support for individuals and groups to express their views and claim their rights – has developed rapidly within the field of social services across the last few years. This is related to the widespread abuse and mistreatment of children and young people in institutional care. However, it is also symbolic of a wider recognition from adults that, due to the continuing imbalance of power and status, children's and young people's voices need to be amplified for them to have any chance of being taken seriously. Similar developments have taken place for disabled people – children and adults – who face difficulties in being respected and taken seriously. Young people themselves have concluded that independent advocacy is an effective mechanism for ensuring their participation rights are acknowledged and put into practice.[4]

POLITICAL CASE FOR CHILDREN'S AND YOUNG PEOPLE'S PARTICIPATION

Children and young people make up about a quarter of the UK's population. Within certain settings – schools, young offender institutions, children's homes and some families – children and young people outnumber adults. Yet the amount of national resources and positive political attention given to children and young people is disproportionately small both to their numbers and to the importance of childhood.[5] The political arguments for children's and young people's participation are threefold.

First, participation engenders positive and respectful relationships between young and old. It fosters respect for human rights, and breaks down barriers and prejudice. Through participation, children and young people can learn about the needs and rights of others, and the importance of mutual respect, compromise and negotiation.

The next generations of adults must be brought up to respect the integrity and dignity of all other human beings, including the small ones, as equal although different from themselves. In exercising participation rights, they are learning the general rules of human rights as well as of democracy.[6]

Second, encouraging children and young people to participate in decisions gives them a stake in their living environments and local communities, thereby reducing conflict.[7]

Finally, participation in childhood is a necessary stepping stone to adult responsibilities and decision-making: positive experiences early in life, especially in relation to community involvement, can engender affiliation to the political process and reduce cynicism and apathy later on.

SOCIAL CASE FOR CHILDREN'S AND YOUNG PEOPLE'S PARTICIPATION

Children and young people are members of every community. As human beings they have automatic and justifiable claims on society, including the right to be regarded and treated with equal worth and status as other people.

SIZE MATTERS: THE PHYSICAL ENVIRONMENT

It is easy for adults to forget that communities partly belong to, and are shaped by, children and young people. For example, nearly all buildings and facilities for the 'general public', with the exception of toilets for wheelchair users, have been designed using the height and strength of the average adult as the norm. That there will always be people of small stature and limited strength seems to have escaped the attention of public architects and planners.

This aspect of children's social exclusion is often defended on the grounds that childhood is something most people grow out of. In fact, many people react with amusement and derision to proposals for adapting physical environments to suit children's needs. They question the point of investing resources and energy into making fundamental changes when babies and children grow so quickly. But this is a narrow and partial approach to community development, investing only in the most powerful section of the community, rather than the whole.

The physical world communicates a great deal about the assumed worth and value of people. Until the end of the 20th century, it was extremely uncommon to see wheelchair users shopping in supermarkets, borrowing books in libraries or waiting in bus queues. Although progress has been extremely slow, legislation now requires new buildings and all public services, including transport, to be made accessible to disabled citizens. Changing the physical environment is seen as an integral part of tackling discrimination against disabled people.

Imagine if the needs of babies and children counted when buildings and public facilities were being designed:

... with doors that they can open safely, handles on their level, child-sized furniture and windows at their height.[8]

If social spaces were seen as belonging to all members of the public – young and old – noisy, playful children would be welcomed on trains and buses. Free play areas would be scattered around shopping complexes, and cars would not be allowed to interfere with street games or bikes and scooters. Shop owners would welcome, not restrict, their young customers. There would be plenty of places for teenagers to socialise, both indoors and outside. Kerbs and doorways would accommodate pushchairs and prams. Community resources such as schools, libraries and leisure centres would be jointly managed by children and young people, with access all day long, seven days a week. Responses to youth crime would be humane and progressive, with politicians encouraging positive relationships between generations rather than playing on fear and mistrust.

VALUING CHILDHOOD IN THE HERE AND NOW

Even though the day-to-day experiences of children and young people are beset with messages that they do not belong, adults invest great hope in children as future caretakers of the planet, carrying precious knowledge, family traditions and cultures into the future. Children and young people are seen as vital to the wellbeing and positive development of families, local communities and nations. Indeed, most cultures define families by the existence of babies and children. Falling birth rates, and decreasing numbers of children in local communities, are usually viewed with alarm and concern. The singular focus on the future role of children can sometimes be a distraction from the here and now of their existence. However, the huge contribution that babies, children and young people make to social life, and to the future of humanity, needs to be constantly remembered and treasured.

Promoting children's and young people's participation helps to counter their invisibility as people. It brings their needs and views to the regular attention of adults, and helps transform negative attitudes and behaviour. Increased visibility should lead us away from seeing children as people-in-the-making, simply passing time until they enter adulthood, towards respecting them as complete human beings with needs, feelings and evolving capacities from the moment they are born.

HOW DID WE GET HERE? AN ANALYSIS OF WHY CHILDREN ARE EXCLUDED

Children's and young people's exclusion from decision-making cannot be tackled effectively without understanding the causes. The proliferation of glossy manuals, handbooks and guides on listening to children and young people that have appeared over the last five years has brought many benefits for children. However, these practical aids can sometimes obscure crucial questions about children's status and lack of power, and the need for wider societal change.

Questions about children's and young people's participation and social inclusion can only be partially understood by reflecting on their social status and position as young people in society. The effects of class, sex, race and disability inequality are also critical to understanding and supporting their meaningful participation in decision-making. Children and young people are not a homogenous group: although age discrimination can be a unifying feature, the existence of poverty and racism, for example, creates huge differences in their lives and opportunities, both across the UK and globally.

The exclusion of children and young people, just like all other forms of discrimination, feeds off negative attitudes and belief systems. To include children and young people successfully in all aspects of society, our basic thinking and fundamental values need to be unearthed, shaken and cast aside if rotten.

Priscilla Alderson uses the work of philosopher Mary Midgley to explain why examining basic values is central to promoting young children's participation rights:

> All beliefs and patterns of thinking have been compared with plumbing... They tend to be invisible and ignored until something goes obviously wrong, such as leaks or blockages. Then people realise how vitally their lives are affected by the hidden pipes (or beliefs), and see that the most practical thing to do is sort out the (mental) plumbing.[9]

Checklists or clever formulae cannot achieve the long-term social inclusion of children and young people, although they can support one-off initiatives and specific projects. Their strength is in *getting people started*. However, sustained change can only come through tackling the root causes of children's and young people's exclusion. We shall now consider possible reasons for their continued invisibility in decision-making processes, split crudely between issues relating to individual children and to individual adults.

Children as the source of the problem	Adults as the source of the problem
• Children and young people do not have the competence to make decisions.	• Adults do not know how to include children.
• Children need to be protected from decision-making.	• Adults fear losing control.
• Children do not want to be included.	• Adults want to be in charge and do not want to include children.

CHILDREN AS THE SOURCE OF THE PROBLEM

The exclusion of children and young people from decision-making processes is frequently justified on the grounds that they do not have the competence or interest to take part, and that they need to be protected from the harshness of adult decision-making.

The competence question

The reality of children's and young people's lives, in the UK and across the globe, is that they are far more competent than adults give them credit for.

Competence is socially constructed: society has expectations about what people can and cannot do; these expectations change over time, and differ between societies and cultures. For example, in the UK political participation was seen as a threat to women's femininity, preventing them from gaining equal voting rights with men until 1928.

The best way of dismantling arguments that children's and young people's competence is a fixed, measurable truth is to consider the expectations and experiences of previous generations.

Modern notions of childhood are said to date from the 16th century, after which education slowly began to dislodge young people from the world of work, politics and sexuality.[10] Even in more recent years, we can see how children's lives and choices have been greatly affected by social and technological change. In 1971, 86 per cent of primary age children went to school by themselves. By 1990, only 29 per cent of children in the same age range were travelling to school without the company of an adult.[11] Ten years later, young children are routinely seen as unable to deal with traffic or other daily hazards that, only a generation earlier, were a normal part of everyday life. The mass production of cars, increased numbers of working parents and media coverage of attacks on children by strangers all contribute to less independent mobility for children.

That expectations and behavioural norms differ greatly across societies is further evidence that the competence to carry out tasks and make decisions is socially rather than biologically determined. Iran has a voting age of 15 years, and seven other countries allow 16- and 17-year-olds to vote. The age at which children are deemed to be responsible for criminal actions is seven in 20 countries across the world. In England and Wales, ten-year-olds are treated as criminally responsible, while in Belgium, Mexico and Uruguay, the age is 18. The law permits heterosexual relationships at 14 in Iceland, 16 in England in Wales and 18 in India.

Even a cursory glance at children's and young people's experiences reveals high levels of responsibility, difficult choices and everyday challenges. Children and young people, even in the affluent UK, often live in perilous conditions:

- One in three under-18-year-olds lives in poverty.
- Institutional racism, including in schools, has now been officially acknowledged.
- Nearly one in four children is affected by divorce before their 16th birthday.
- The Department of Health estimates that there are between 19,000 and 51,000 young carers in England alone. These are under-18-year-olds who have caring and domestic responsibilities above and beyond normal household chores.
- Each year, 100,000 children and young people miss school through injury or illness.
- Over 30,000 children were on child protection registers across England in the year up to 31 March 2000.
- More than a million children have called ChildLine since its lines opened in October 1986.
- Between one and two children a week in the UK die at the hands of their parents; the vast majority are babies.

The myth of the happy childhood, where children can skip along without care or responsibility, ignores the daily grind on many children's lives of bereavement, family conflict, school stress and bullying. Global issues such as war, pollution and religious intolerance all take their toll on babies and children.

But even if many children's and young people's lives were not a patchwork of challenges and dangers, their participation rights would nevertheless remain. Young human beings should not have to live through adversity to prove that they are competent and can exercise choices.

Rather than expecting children and young people to jump through the competency hoop, a more positive approach would be to adopt the working principle that all children and young people have the capacity to contribute to all decision-making that affects them. The scope of decision-making, and level of influence accorded to children's and young people's wishes and views, would be measured by their understanding and individual capacities. But their views would not count for less just because of their chronological age.

Finally, it is important to remember that the ability to make decisions can only come through practice. Experience of being respected and taken seriously is crucial to children developing, over time, the skills and confidence to make decisions, not just about their own lives but also about their wider community. The earlier children are allowed choices, the better:

> If children are not allowed to make decisions because they have no experience of decision-making, how do they ever get started? This is Catch 22.[12]

Protecting childhood

The concept and everyday practice of children's rights suffers from enormous misunderstanding and distortion. Arguments for children to be treated with the same respect and worth as adults become seriously muddled in translation. Proponents of children's rights, rather than being seen as respectable and credible human rights campaigners, are mocked and accused of trying to make children into miniature adults. Critics argue that too much responsibility and decision-making robs children and young people of their childhood. They also claim that the concept and practice of children's rights encourages poor behaviour and selfishness. Images of children filing for parental divorce because their pocket money allowances are too low prevail. Many other red herrings are held up in an effort to discredit and slow down progress on realising children's human rights. In his comprehensive review of safeguards for children living away from home, Sir William Utting discussed the myths that prevail about the Children Act 1989:

> Mention of children's rights provokes a sour response in some quarters, along the lines that the Children Act destroyed parental authority to control and discipline children... The Children Act does not say that children must always have their own way, or that they must always be believed. Such loose attributions are made by adults grasping for excuses for welching on their responsibilities to children.[13]

Continuing to exclude children from decision-making is not a sign of respect for their youth or for their relative lack of life experience.

Rather, it disregards their basic human need to be valued and treated with importance. It also misses the vital point that children have evolving capacities which shape how they express their views and wishes, and determine the level and type of influence they have. For example, it would be wasteful to send babies questionnaires on improvements to local play parks but their preferences could be observed by watching them at play and elicited through contact with their parents, carers or older siblings.

Promoting participation in decision-making can add to children's protection. Children's participation is an integral part of the Government's five-year programme to transform children's services, especially the care system. There is now widespread acknowledgement that children's and young people's safety in the care system relies on them being listened to and involved in decisions, both about their own lives and also in general policy and service development. Linked with this is the role of complaints procedures in ensuring that children are taken seriously when they express concerns about their care and treatment, or disclose abuse. The Waterhouse Tribunal into the historical abuse of children in care in Wales heard grave accounts of abused and mistreated children in care having nowhere to turn to:

> Over and over again victims of abuse told the Tribunal that they did not know how to make a formal complaint against a member of staff; and [senior mangers] conceded that no such procedures were laid down. The higher management of the Social Services Department simply did not recognise the existence of the problem.[14]

Finally, discussions about children's rights and protection often uncover basic fears that children and young people will be left to make decisions that are harmful to themselves or others. The context for human rights, including children's human rights, is society. Social responsibility for others, and personal responsibility for the consequences of actions and decisions, are part of the human rights package. In this respect, recognising that children have human rights does not lead to a state of *laissez faire* or non-intervention. The question of whether to force a young child to wear a coat to school will, for instance, be based on a calculation of the harm caused by compelling her to wear clothing she sees as restrictive, compared with the chance of her catching a cold.[15] More complex decisions, for example, about where and with whom children and young people should live, also have to explore the consequences of refusing to act on their wishes and feelings. Whenever decisions are made that affect children and young people, it is important not only to seek their views and ideas but also to explain what has been decided and why, giving them the space and opportunity to question and challenge, if necessary.

The right not to take part
The debate about whether children and young people are interested in making decisions is an important one. It raises concerns about them being forced into activities against their wishes. This, of course, is an anathema to respecting children's human rights. Genuine participatory initiatives and approaches are always based on the practice of informed consent. This is where children and young people are given full and accessible information about the decision in question, or the proposed project or activity. They will be regularly reminded that they do not have to take part, and given choices about how, where and when to express their views and ideas. Importantly, children and young people should be reassured that non-participation will not affect how they are treated. When group activities are being planned, different types and levels of involvement can be offered: for example, children and young people can take part as observers, or take on other roles such as note-taker, project photographer or video operator.

It is also important to examine why children and young people may be reluctant to take part in initiatives to get their voices heard and opinions acted on. They may have poor experience of adults listening to them, or of taking them seriously. They may lack self-esteem and confidence because they are bullied and ridiculed at home or in school. Their personal circumstances may prevent them being involved in activities over a period of time, perhaps because they constantly move home, or because they have caring responsibilities, or even because they expect to be given a custodial sentence for past offending. Many young people also see the inevitability of growing out of childhood as a reason for not investing too much energy and time in trying to change the way society treats children and young people. The length of time it can take adults to make any substantial change feeds into this. A teenager who wants his right to self-expression to be respected within school can, for example, end up making a pragmatic calculation that positive results will only come after his formal education is over. This affirms the importance of achieving short-term 'hits', even if the more substantial goals of participatory projects and initiatives take years to materialise.[16]

ADULTS AS THE SOURCE OF THE PROBLEM

Adults have the unique power to encourage or crush babies' and children's basic need for self-expression, and evolving capacity to make decisions. In 1994, the United Nations International Year of the Family recognised the unique role of parents and carers in respecting and promoting children's human rights. The slogan for the year was:

Building the smallest democracy at the heart of society.

Although modern parenting guides now stress the need to respect and listen to babies and children, there is a pervading belief in our society that children are not people in their own right, and that adults always know best. Even though parents and carers are encouraged to listen, laws and policies give children only partial rights in certain situations. Listening to children, and respecting and seriously taking into account their views and ideas, continues to be seen as a matter of personal choice. Children's basic human right to participate in society, as expressed in the UNCRC, is left to the goodwill of individuals. In families, while children continue to have limited rights in domestic law to participate and parental responsibilities remain undefined in law, the promotion of children's fundamental human rights continues to be seen as optional – as a parenting style rather than the birthright of all babies and children.

Adults don't know what to do

Even when adults decide they do want to support positively children's and young people's participation and social inclusion, they often have fears and doubts about their capabilities and the consequences of promoting children's rights. This is especially the case for those working in institutions such as schools, hospitals or in social work and community development, where wider cultural change is part of the solution to children's and young people's social exclusion.

It is not surprising that children's human rights, including their right to participate in all decisions that affect them, is still a new subject to many professionals. Article 42 of the UNCRC states that governments must do all they can to promote awareness of the standards and principles of the Convention. The Committee on the Rights of the Child recommends that training courses should include teaching on children's human rights. A decade has lapsed since the UK Government pledged to fully implement the UNCRC. Yet there has not been one single piece of Government guidance for any professional group on how to promote and respect children's Convention rights. Social work, nursing, teaching and probation courses still routinely omit to mention the UNCRC, and hardly register the international requirement to take into account children's views whenever making decisions. If the theory of children's participation has not reached the syllabuses of professional training programmes, it is little wonder that most adults struggle with the practicalities. Even when children's rights are included in training courses, discussions are often squeezed into a half-day session, sometimes with an external guest speaker. This relegates children's human rights to that of a special 'topic' rather than an over-arching commitment to children. Newly-qualified teachers and social workers often complain that their courses have ill-equipped them to communicate effectively with children and young people, either individually or in groups. There is a further pressing need to support the contribution of children and young people in adult training courses. Some social work courses now routinely invite care leavers to advise students on the care system, but this approach has not widened to other areas of social work, or to teacher or medical training, for example.

Although professional training courses are on the whole still strangers to the theory and practice of children's human rights, in recent years there has been a steady growth of publications and training materials aimed at policy-makers and practitioners in child protection, health, local communities, the care system and education. A charter of participation has been developed, based on the direct experiences of young people involved in rights and participation work.[17] Standards have been prepared for young people's participation in local government.[18] Oxfordshire's Children's Rights Commissioner, managed by Save the Children but financed by the County Council and supported by other statutory service providers across Oxfordshire, has developed a 'children's rights checklist'. The checklist asks everyone who plans or delivers services that affect children and young people to:

- think about children's rights in relation to the service they are providing;
- seek and act on the views of children and young people;
- be able to show that children's rights are reflected in the way that their organisation works with children and young people.

There are many practical steps organisations can take to promote children's human rights, as shown in Table 2 opposite.

Adults fear losing control

The biggest anxiety that adults have when embarking on initiatives that respect children's rights is losing control, and taking unacceptable risks.

It is true that working with, rather than against, children and young people will involve giving up power and control. But this is not a recipe for chaos and irresponsible behaviour: the sky will not fall down because adults treat children with respect. There is a common misconception that children and young people are uniquely incapable of deferring their own needs in favour of others. Aside from the fact that adults are capable of huge greed and selfishness, the reality is that respectful and participatory relationships will, in time, lead to more giving and receiving, not less. Just as starving people will over-eat when first presented with food, children and young people who have previously been disrespected and excluded from decision-making may initially have an exaggerated need to be validated

Table 2 Promoting participation in organisations that work with children and young people

The TO DO list
• Make sure information about the UNCRC, and your organisation's commitment to children's and young people's participation rights, is included in all recruitment material, including job advertisements and information to applicants.
• Include information on the duty to promote and support children's participation rights in all job descriptions and staff contracts.
• Help children and young people to be directly involved in staff recruitment processes. This will test the suitability and skills of applicants while giving a positive message about your organisation's practical commitment to children's and young people's participation.
• Include meetings with children and young people in the induction process of all new staff.
• Ensure supervisors and managers routinely address children's and young people's participation in decision-making through supervision and staff meetings.
• Build feedback from children and young people into staff appraisal systems.
• Provide detailed guidance, developed in partnership with children and young people, on the responsibilities of staff and managers to promote and respect children's and young people's participation rights.
• Develop in-house training courses on children's rights and participation.
• Invest in information systems that collect data on children's and young people's participation, both in decision-making processes about them as individuals (e.g. review meetings in care and school admission and exclusion panels) and in general policy and service development (e.g. involvement in staff recruitment panels and training).
• Ensure all policy or practice proposals that affect children and young people are assessed as to the likely consequences (this process has been called 'child-proofing').
• Support innovative projects and approaches to meeting children's and young people's needs; set aside dedicated budgets for young people-led projects and activities.
• Ensure children and young people have access to independent information, advice and advocacy so that they can find out about and claim their human rights.

as people. The same is true for other groups of people who, historically, have been ignored. The challenge is to build environments and communities where all human rights are respected so that no person, of whatever age or size, feels they must trample on others to be heard. Children and young people are usually very understanding about the slowness of organisational change and what, realistically, can be achieved. The key to positive working relationships is honesty and information, and not raising expectations too high.

Just as children and young people develop their skills and confidence to participate in decisions through practice, adults also need to experiment and find out for themselves that participatory ways of working with, and relating to, children and young people can bring enormous practical change and pleasure. They can start by making small adjustments in their behaviour; perhaps deciding to cut down on the number of times they say "No" to a child they live with, and replacing this with more open dialogue such as "Why do you ask that?" or "Please tell me more because I don't understand." Adults can think about the everyday decisions they make that affect children's and young people's lives, and explore the level and extent of children's and young people's involvement. They can then move on to inviting children and young people to advise them on how they can work or live in ways that respect, rather than curtail, children's participation rights. As their confidence grows, adults can gradually learn to support children and young people in taking more control over decisions and projects, taking a back seat wherever possible and appropriate.

Different levels of children's and young people's participation are often represented by what has been termed the 'ladder of participation'. Sherry Arnstein first developed the concept in 1969 in relation to citizen involvement in housing and community development in the USA (see page 49).[19] It has since been adapted for children's participation by Roger Hart for the United Nations Children's Fund (UNICEF).[20] The ladder has eight rungs. The top five rungs depict genuine participation, although in different degrees. The bottom three non-participatory rungs include activities such as asking children and young people for their views when decisions have already been made, or holding competitions for children to design their ideal school or hospital but giving no feedback on how their ideas will be used, other than for the decoration of corridors and hallways. Another regular activity that gets mistaken for worthwhile participation is inviting young people to sing or read poetry at

The ladder of participation

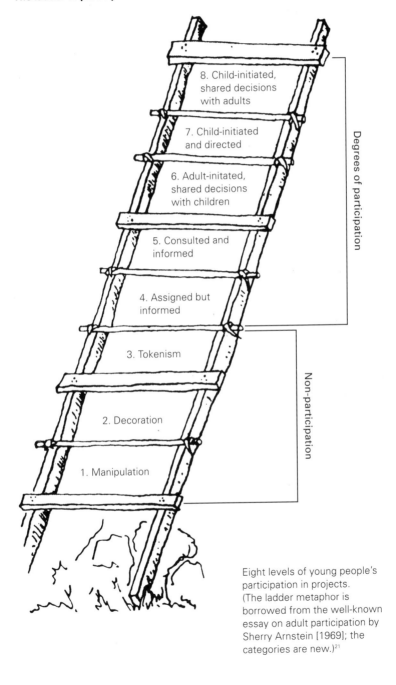

8. Child-initiated, shared decisions with adults

7. Child-initiated and directed

6. Adult-initated, shared decisions with children

5. Consulted and informed

4. Assigned but informed

3. Tokenism

2. Decoration

1. Manipulation

Degrees of participation

Non-participation

Eight levels of young people's participation in projects. (The ladder metaphor is borrowed from the well-known essay on adult participation by Sherry Arnstein [1969]; the categories are new.)[21]

conferences without giving them full and accessible information about the purpose and style of the event, or the chance to take part in other ways.

Although the ladder metaphor has been widely criticised for its simplicity, it is nevertheless useful in pointing to the need to be vigilant about the true extent of participation and choice in activities and projects supposedly designed to empower children and young people.

Adults don't want to change

Some adults blankly refuse to change, preferring to carry around second-hand beliefs that they are superior, and that there is no place for children in decision-making. They hold onto their power, and feel no shame for the terrible way that they treat children:

> *I have a problem with my stepdad... he comes up to me, like, I'll go into my bedroom and I'll back off and I'll shut the door, and he goes "Don't shut the door" and I'm like "Oh God, he's going to hit me or something"... Many times before he's hit me round the head, and like [I'll say] "You've got no right to hit me, you have no right to have a go at me", and then he says, he keeps telling me "I have every right to... I'm an adult, I can do whatever I want... you're only a kid. Sorry you can't do nothing: you're only a kid. You have no right to do anything."* [22]

Reluctant or oppressive adults need re-educating so that they can become a positive force and influence in children's and young people's lives. Legal reform is one major way of slowly changing attitudes. For example, in the case of parental physical punishment, attitudes in Sweden have changed dramatically since smacking was banned in 1979. In 1965, 53 per cent of Swedes agreed with corporal punishment; now only 11 per cent think it has a place in the family. Furthermore, only 6 per cent of under-35-year-olds in Sweden now agree with any form of physical punishment. [23]

Legal reform is central to raising the status of children and young people, giving them full protection from assault and also, crucially, a legal right to be consulted on all decisions that significantly affect them. In the meantime, organisations that employ adults who have out-of-date attitudes towards children have a responsibility to help them change or, ultimately, they must assist them to seek more appropriate employment.

BREAKING DOWN THE VICTIM MENTALITY: HOW ADULTS CAN RESPECT CHILDREN

Adults have many roles and relationships with children and young people: most of these carry huge amounts of authority and responsibility. It is extremely rare for adults and children to have relationships based purely on friendship or mutual support. There usually has to be a purpose for connections between young and old, with adults setting out to socialise, educate, rescue, treat, cure or reform children and young people. Underlying all these activities is the belief that children are lacking vital human ingredients, and only adult intervention can save them.

A view of the child's mind and body as temporary, and relatively worthless, pervades the history of childhood.[24]

Of course, adults have much to pass on to children and young people: that we have lived longer should mean we have accumulated useful knowledge and wisdom. But each interaction with children and young people does not have to involve the passing of one-way information or instruction. Children and young people also have lots to teach adults: about their own experiences; about childhood and youth culture; and about all the things they as individuals know that individual adults don't. They can also help adults develop as people, encouraging mutual respect, negotiation, patience and acceptance of diversity. Most, if given the chance, will rekindle in adults the ability to have fun and enjoy life.

For children's participation rights to be truly respected, adults have to move away from seeing children simply as beneficiaries or victims. The following principles for effective participation are a useful starting point.

Principles for effective participation: making a reality of Article 12 of the UN Convention on the Rights of the Child

- All children and young people have the right to be involved in decisions that affect them.
- All children and young people can express their views and ideas.
- Children and young people should, wherever possible, be able to decide when, where and how they take part in decision-making.
- The way children and young people are seen and treated affects how much they can participate.
- Children and childhood are just as important as adults and adulthood.
- Never assume that decisions are too small to matter or too big for children and young people to handle.
- Making space for children and young people benefits everyone.
- Children and young people have the right to take part in decision-making today, tomorrow and every day.

GET INVOLVED FOR A CHANGE: ACTING ON CHILDREN'S AND YOUNG PEOPLE'S IDEAS AND VIEWS

Listening to children is not some politically correct mantra to be recited but never acted upon. Nor is it a sop designed to pacify children so that adults can go on controlling young lives with clearer consciences… Listening should in future be seen as a fundamental form of social inclusion, capable of showing children that they matter and belong. More than that, it is the all-important means by which adults will improve their understanding of what children are really feeling, thereby finding more effective ways of responding to their needs.[25]

Adults need to ask some hard questions about the purpose and impact of participatory ways of working. How much positive change for children has resulted from the new emphasis on listening to children, and promoting their participation, within public services, and further afield? What impact is all this talk about participation and empowerment having on day-to-day relationships between adults and children? Peter Newell, in considering the place of children and young people in neighbourhoods, questions what has really changed for children since the almost universal ratification of the UNCRC, and concludes that:

So far most of this progress is paper progress, words on paper.[26]

Paper progress does not, on the whole, impress children and young people. They base their judgements on real life. An organisation may have a framed mission statement on the wall espousing its commitment to tackling bullying and racism. But the day-to-day experiences of children and young people may tell a different story. That is why the impact of policies and service developments can only be rigorously tested through engagement with real children and young people.

That each new piece of research or consultation report on children's and young people's views stresses that they don't feel listened to or respected by adults is testimony that there is a long way to go. Even in the care system, where children's rights have been on the agenda since the late 1970s, children and young people still routinely complain that staff and managers do not take them seriously.

WHY PARTICIPATION?

This is not to end on a downbeat note: the case studies that follow clearly show that positive and lasting change can come with determination, effort and collaboration between young and old. However, it does point to the need for honest soul-searching from all those working with children and young people for sustainable change, in individual lives as well as in wider society. There are three leading questions in addressing the purpose and impact of promoting participation.

WHO BENEFITS?

The first is the question of *who benefits* from participation. Who personally gains from being involved; and how do these gains compare between adults and children? Who has the most fun; who gets to be treated more seriously; who learns and develops their skills; and whose status is enhanced by taking part? Are participatory initiatives established to change the lives of individual children and young people, or to influence national and local public policy-making? How important is positive publicity for individual projects and organisations; who gets a chance to determine projects and activities; and would your organisation run projects rooted in young people's experiences and views, for example, related to drugs or school reform, that may attract negative publicity?

WHAT PERSONAL CHANGE?

The second theme is centred on *personal change*. How much personal change do adults and children make; whose attitudes and ideas are challenged; and who learns new ways of listening and communicating? Who gets to find out how different people make decisions; who allows themselves to experiment, and takes the risk of looking or sounding inexperienced; and, crucially, who transfers their new ideas and knowledge to relationships at home?

WHAT DO CHILDREN AND YOUNG MAKE OF IT?

Finally, we come to the biggest question of all, *what do children and young people make of it?* If children and young people were asked, what would they say about the motivations of your organisation, or you personally, for promoting participation? How discernible would the activities and approaches of your organisation be from others less openly committed to children's rights and participation? What would children and young people rate as success; what advice would they give you about progressing further; and what would they tell you to stop doing? If children and young people were given encouragement and support to tell you exactly what they want and need, how much would your organisation have to change and how much would you be prepared to give?

Case studies

S ix case studies have been chosen to represent different models and approaches that The Children's Society uses to promote children's and young people's participation.

The case studies are united by their common aim of promoting the rights of children and young people to participate in and influence decision-making processes. In some respects they all tell the same story of adults seeking new ways of working in partnership with children and young people. In addition to this common theme, each case study has something different and special to share. Difficulties and successes are explored equally.

The first two case studies show the challenges of trying to change systems so that they can become more responsive to the needs and rights of children and young people. They are:

- the Genesis school inclusion project;
- the UCAN advocacy project.

The next case study focuses on a creative way of consulting children and young people while also describing ways in which young carers have been supported to influence developments in policy and practice. That is:

- the young carers' festivals.

The fourth case study examines how The Children's Society has supported young disabled people to claim their participation rights. It is:

- Ask Us! – young disabled people get active.

The final two case studies share the pitfalls and triumphs of trying to achieve long-term organisational change. They are:

- Small voices count too – challenges in consulting and taking young children seriously;
- The Liverpool Bureau for Children and Young People.

Each study provides background information on the development and work of the project, together with an analysis of what worked and lessons learned. Factual project information was obtained from annual reports, funding proposals, promotional materials, and research and consultation reports. In addition, managers and staff met with the author to reflect on the history and activities of their projects. Three of the six case studies further benefit from the reflections and insights of children and young people who are, or have been, involved in the projects.

Respecting the whole child: the Genesis school inclusion project

It helps a lot of students to stay in school because sometimes people think they are alone. And inside they feel empty. If they have people who love them, really care and understand them, they will be able to share what is bothering them so they can be happy like a normal child.[1]

HOW THE PROJECT BEGAN

In 1994, a reverend of a church in the Peckham area of London went into The Children's Society regional office. He explained that he was a chair of governors of a local secondary school that was experiencing many difficulties associated with children's social and economic circumstances. The school had recently been inspected by OFSTED whose report confirmed, among other things, the negative impact of poverty on students' educational achievement.

Staff from the school and The Children's Society began to explore how they could work together to support educational inclusion. They decided to make available a dedicated area of the building where school students could approach The Children's Society for advice and support at any time on any matter relating to their educational experience. The plan was to have "a walk-in ChildLine based in school".

I actually think that if [the project staff] weren't there that kids would have more anger in them and there'd be more fights, because if people feel that they really hate someone and want to punch them they go and talk to [Genesis].

A FRESH START

Initially the project was called 'The Children's Society school project'. Soon after settling into the school, staff from the project carried out a survey among students to find a more suitable name. A 14-year-old suggested the name 'Genesis' because of its association with a new beginning.

Over the five years that the Genesis project ran in this first school, staff had over 3,000 contacts with children and young people. They ran support groups, met students individually to discuss family difficulties and gave young people advice on their rights and the law. Further, they facilitated classroom discussions and workshops on topical issues, and provided training for teachers on communicating with and understanding the challenges faced by students. The emphasis was on listening to individual children and young people, and working with them to address difficulties in school. As one young person explained:

The Children's Society helps children stay in school. They show them that education is important in life and also that children are more free. They can achieve something, a goal. They have people to listen to their problems and have someone who is going to be there. They don't even have to phone; they can just knock on the door.

TEACHER SUPPORT

Staff involved in the early days of the project felt that most teachers were neutral. Very few positively supported the project, while some were overtly critical, seeing it as a 'soft option'. For example, one member of staff believed that any child or young person caught breaking any of the school rules should be excluded immediately. A senior teacher once remarked to a project worker that she should bear in mind that the area was Peckham and that children needed to get used to living in this type of environment. At times, it seemed that teacher expectations were lower than those of the students. Notably, from approximately 80 teaching staff, only about five lived in the local area, perhaps reflecting a lack of engagement with children's and young people's day-to-day lives.

MAKING A POSITIVE DIFFERENCE

Despite the doubts of some teaching staff, the value of the Genesis project was evident from the beginning. Students came to the project at times of crisis or when they wanted a listening ear to talk through a problem in confidence, as well as when they just needed a quiet space to complete some homework. One recent school leaver saw a member of the project's staff team in the street. He had heard from his sibling that the project was about to close in his old school, and said:

> They're gonna lose it. The only thing that's holding the school together is that project.

At the project's farewell party, the school caretaker said that Genesis had led to a remarkable change in students' behaviour. He even concluded that the five-year period of the project had been the best of his 15 years working at the school.

The Children's Society's project in Peckham was probably the first example of its kind in the country, pioneering a new type of student support as well as promoting partnership working between the statutory and voluntary sectors. Even today, when many schools have outside agencies coming in regularly, it is rare to have a voluntary organisation housed within a school.

While the benefits of the project were visible from the start for the children and young people who needed someone to turn to when pressures at home or school became intolerable, this first school-based project also had its difficulties.

SUCCESS IS MORE THAN EXAM RESULTS

As time progressed, the school was increasingly under pressure to raise educational standards. This led to the headteacher (the third in four years) placing expectations on the Genesis project that ran counter to its ethos. For example, there was a request for project staff to become involved in undertaking assessments of special educational needs. Previously it had been accepted that the project's role was to support children and young people through the process rather than to be formally involved.

The rate of fixed-term exclusions also started to rise: rather than back the project to support children and young people, the school now tolerated the exclusion of students who threatened its academic performance. This was at odds with the raison d'être of the Genesis project – to promote educational inclusion for all.

At the end of the five years, The Children's Society decided not to pursue a further partnership with the school. It was felt that the exclusive focus on academic attainment was incompatible with the project's inclusive approach.

There are two major learning points from the period leading up to The Children's Society decision not to extend its partnership. The first relates to the pivotal role that senior managers play in building or blocking an organisation's commitment to children's rights and participation. The early success of the Genesis project was severely compromised by the arrival of a headteacher whose focus was different from her predecessors: this underlines the need constantly to communicate the value of participatory approaches to key stakeholders.

The second point relates to the capacity and willingness of voluntary organisations that run participatory projects to negotiate their way out of difficulties. It seems that the problems in this school were left to staff at project level to resolve. As this approach was clearly unsuccessful, questions remain about whether senior managers from The Children's Society could have approached the headteacher and school governors formally to make the case for continuing the project. That a single individual, albeit holding a very powerful position, was able to undermine a project that was so obviously valued by children and young people, raises issues about the responsibility and capacity of large organisations to support effectively innovative and challenging work on the ground. More positively, the project leader reports that the difficulties experienced in this first school has led to a sharper focus when agreeing the terms of partnerships at the beginning of new school-based projects.

PARTNERS IN CHANGE: WHAT'S IMPORTANT?

The Children's Society's Genesis project is now working in three secondary schools in South London. One is an all girls' school; all are in multicultural areas and each school has over 900 students. In addition to funds from The Children's Society, financial support for the project comes from the Department for Education and Skills, a local Health Action Zone and various trust funds. So what helps the project to achieve its goal of promoting educational inclusion?

STUDENT-CENTRED

The approach used by the Genesis project is flexible according to the needs and priorities of students. For instance, in one of the three schools, there are more male than female students. This has led to problems of boys dominating classroom discussions and taking up a lot of physical space. Project staff have therefore facilitated groups for girls to talk about their school experiences, and to develop their confidence and assertiveness.

INFLUENCING POLICY AND PRACTICE

Although the project's focus is primarily on supporting individuals, staff have also helped children and young people to influence general matters of policy and service development. This is extremely important if organisations and institutions are to become truly child-centred: supporting individual children and young people to tackle individual difficulties and problems in school is valuable in itself but this will not, on its own, change how schools are run.

The Genesis project sees the establishment of school councils as fundamental to promoting educational inclusion. Project staff work in partnership with schools to provide training for students on the role and function of school councils, and they support them in running effective meetings and contribute positively to decision-making. A familiar issue was raised in one of the school councils – the poor condition of student toilets. As a result, students from Years 7 and 8 (12- and 13-year-olds) prepared a proposal for the redecoration of their toilets. The headteacher accepted the students' suggestions, and the toilets are now markedly improved. They have been painted, and there are mirrors on the wall and locks on each of the cubicle doors.

The project engenders responsibility and positive participation in school life in other ways. For example, project staff in one school encouraged Year 11 students to organise an end-of-year trip, and the young people made all the hotel and travel arrangements. Students took part in the school's Citizenship Day: they ran a cake stall and put the proceeds towards the trip.

The project also supports peer-mentoring programmes and gets involved in Personal, Social and Health Education whole class/group teaching on topical subjects, such as relationships, bullying and sex education.

Two younger students, who attend a young carers' group run by the Genesis project, describe with enthusiasm their efforts to organise a talent contest. They wanted to raise money to pay for a trip for members of the young carers' group. Although they spent several weeks planning the event, in the end it didn't go ahead because of conflict within the group. However, this did not diminish the students' sense of pride and achievement at being allowed to run such an important event.

We had a file that thick. We learned that we could actually organise stuff. We also learned that everyone needs to work together to make it happen... Before, you couldn't trust a teacher but now I know they will listen to you properly.

STAFF ATTITUDES AND SKILLS

Project staff are from a mixture of professional backgrounds, including youth work, further education teaching, counselling, educational welfare and community-based social work. When the project manager recruits staff, he always looks for the following characteristics:

- respect for children and young people;
- empathy with young people's circumstances and the challenges they face;
- driven by young people's needs and interests;
- able to hear what young people have to say, rather than telling them how to feel or behave;
- flexible approach but able to maintain firm professional boundaries;
- committed to challenging discrimination wherever it occurs;
- interested in and committed to positive youth development;
- enjoys and likes being with young people.

WORKING TOGETHER

There is an emphasis upon partnership working, making links and bringing in other professionals to assist children and young people when necessary. In one school, a whole range of agencies are available to provide information and advice to students. This includes a local credit union, a sex education counsellor, and a nurse and drugs counsellor. As one young person put it:

All the things to do with out-of-school life.

Another young person said:

I think it's really good the way they're helping young children because they can't really talk to their parents because they don't actually understand. They can actually put you in touch with others you need to talk with.

TOP MARKS FROM STUDENTS

Conversations with students from two of the schools where the Genesis project works were extremely positive. There were three recurring themes. First, the young people felt that project staff were always available for students. They gave examples of being able to use project computers[2] or to come out of lessons if they are distressed or unhappy:

You're always allowed on their computers. There's loads of us who go just to hang out in the breaks.

They'll always make time to talk with you then and there, and if you want to go back they give you an appointment slip and you can get out of your lesson... but not in core subjects like Science and Maths.

Second, students repeatedly stressed the confidential nature of the project:

We know that we can talk to anyone in young carers and everyone knows it won't go out of that room. Whatever is said around the table, everyone has their say but it's one of the rules that it doesn't go out.

You can talk about your feelings... and because it's confidential, nobody's going to go out and tell others.

Finally, students felt that the accessibility of the project was greatly enhanced by it being based within a school:

You're more recognised in a school. People always hear about it. Also you get more trust. If you're a new company that's started up, you won't get much trust because they don't know. You may have private rooms but they don't know.

If it weren't in a school, less and less people would go.

You know where to go and you know they'll give you support.

But the students did not restrict their praise to the project staff alone. Their headteachers and other teaching staff also impressed them. They gave examples of a headteacher keeping children and young people up-to-date on national and local current affairs during morning school gatherings. They explained how some of their teachers gave up their free time to help students catch up on work they have missed, or not yet completed. They also noted that:

... teachers don't break confidences.

If you've got a point to get across, they'll always listen.

A CASE FOR INDEPENDENT ADVOCACY?

That the project's focus is on listening to and supporting children and young people raises a question about why it has not extended its services to include independent advocacy for children and young people. There are many areas of school life that independent advocacy could help to address. These include admissions and exclusions, student sanctions, complaints about unfair treatment, and access to educational allowances and school trips and holidays. This kind of development would inevitably alter the emphasis of the project towards achieving change in school policy and practice of schools. Children and young people would still benefit enormously from being valued and taken seriously but, crucially, they would also be supported in channelling their experiences and ideas into proposing and being part of practical changes in their schools.

CHANGING THE EDUCATION SYSTEM: A NEW BEGINNING FOR EVERYONE?

The students' positive attitudes about their school probably indicate that initiatives such as the Genesis project thrive in settings where there is already respect for students, and a commitment to listening to them and supporting them to take part in decision-making. The idea that promoting mutual respect and meaningful participation in schools helps to reduce educational exclusion is also becoming more popular. For example, the Government's Green Paper on schools,[3] published in February 2001, introduced a new concept of 'education with character'.

Schools: building on success
Green Paper, February 2001

- Academic achievement is clearly crucial both to ensure that individuals have a range of options when they finish school and to ensure the future success of society as a whole. But no one believes it is the only important outcome of schooling. It is also important that pupils learn to know right from wrong; to get along with their fellow pupils, whatever their background; to work in teams; to make a contribution to the school as a community; and to develop positive attitudes to life and work... Perhaps the most important means of ensuring pupils develop character in this sense is the ethos of the school they attend. All the evidence suggests that where schools develop a positive, respectful and can-do ethos, not only do pupils develop better as rounded people, they are also likely to achieve higher academic standards.

- [The Government will]... Encourage schools to involve pupils much more actively in decisions, not just about their own individual learning, but about their class and their school as a whole. This can be done through the establishment of school councils, through regular surveys of pupil attitudes and a range of other means.

OFSTED estimates that there are around 100,000 young people in England and Wales a year out of school on fixed-term exclusions: enough to fill more than 160 large secondary schools. The Children's Society is convinced that problems at school are linked to problems at home and to wider society. Pushing children and young people further to the margins does not help them feel valued, or motivate them to chase their dreams. The Genesis project shows that schools are not just places where children and young people learn facts and figures. Students do not leave their lives at the school entrance and pick them back up when they leave. They carry them around with them throughout the day, and sometimes these difficulties can be compounded by school life. A young carer explained, for example, about her friend in primary school having to cope alone with worries about her terminally ill mum:

I reckon it would be very good to [have the Genesis project] in a primary. I knew a young girl whose mum had cancer and the school weren't offering any help at all. When her mum did actually die, there was no support for her. She had to leave her classroom because she was crying.

Educational communities can be transformed by respecting and believing in children and young people, and by ensuring they have people there for them when needed. If children and young people are to develop their personality, talents and mental and physical abilities to their fullest potential, as prescribed by Article 29 of the UNCRC, a truly inclusive approach is required. The Genesis project has helped thousands of children and young people get more out of their school experience. It has shown children and young people that adults do want to listen to them and take them seriously. Further, it has had some success in supporting school students to make changes in their school environment, from refurbishing toilets to tackling bullying. Only time will tell whether this innovative project is part of a new chapter in the history of Britain's education system.

For more information about the Genesis project, please contact:

Simon Hepburn
The Children's Society
91–93 Queens Road
Peckham
London
SE15 2EZ

Tel: 020 7639 1466
E-mail: simon.hepburn@childrenssociety.org.uk

Changing the child protection system: the UCAN advocacy project

HOW THE PROJECT BEGAN

The Children's Society has a long history of supporting families in contact with social services in Gwent. The child protection advocacy project evolved after the organisation had worked for several years with parents, particularly those involved in the child protection system. Once the importance of parental participation was acknowledged and promoted within social services, it was time for The Children's Society to shift its focus towards children's and young people's participation.

> They're always there for you. If you need to talk, they'll be there for you and come down to talk with you even if it's after work. They don't seem like social services. It's like they've known you for ages. Social services try to get you to speak about stuff you don't really want to.[1]

> Advocacy... they like support you. Social workers try and help you to make sure you're safe and all that but advocacy try to guide you and they're there for young people.

The project was established in 1996 and aims to promote the fullest implementation of children's and young people's rights, especially their right to participate and influence decisions that affect them. It supports children and young people involved in the child protection system as well as those who are looked after or attending residential special schools. The project operates at three levels to ensure children's and young people's participation rights are understood and respected:

- in procedures that affect individual children's and young people's lives, such as child protection investigations, meetings and criminal court hearings;
- in influencing local policy and service development affecting children and young people;
- in contributing to national developments that have an impact on children and young people.

In 2000, the project changed its name to UCAN to promote a positive message to children and young people:

They can have a voice, they can take part, they can achieve all kinds of things with the right support and if adults believe in them.[2]

ADVOCACY: THE BASICS

Advocacy is a process of helping people to express themselves and make changes. It is a way of redressing inequalities in power and knowledge. Effective advocacy enables people to have the confidence and information to articulate their views and ideas, and positively influence decision-making. Sometimes advocates speak on behalf of people, but they usually support people to speak for themselves, using whatever form of communication suits them.

Advocates provide information about the law, give guidance about strategies and approaches, and actively encourage people to achieve their goals and wishes.

STAMP OF APPROVAL

Children's and young people's advocacy in social services started in 1987 when Leicestershire County Council appointed the UK's first children's rights officer. It took ten years for this new approach of supporting children and young people in difficulty to gain official recognition. In 1997, Sir William Utting, in his publication on safeguards for children living away from home, noted that:

One of the most beneficial developments of the last decade has been the arrival and gradual development of children's rights services for young people looked after by local authorities.[3]

Less than three years after this seminal report, children's and young people's advocacy was debated in the Houses of Parliament for the first time.[4]

Supporting children and young people to express their views and ideas

The Minister for Health, Lord Hunt, confirmed to Parliament during the passage of the Care Standards Act in January 2000 that:
"Advocacy is about effectively articulating the child's view, right or wrong. It is not about what the advocate thinks is best or in the child's welfare. Advocacy is grounded in Article 12 of the UN Convention on the Rights of the Child, which assures children capable of forming their own views the right to express those views freely in all matters affecting them."

THE CHILDREN FIRST PROGRAMME

The Government's pledge to transform children's social services has greatly assisted the growth of advocacy services. The Welsh Assembly's Children First programme, launched in 1999, initially for three years, stresses the need to listen to and respond to children's views and experiences.

There are 11 objectives to the Children First programme: Objectives 3 and 9 have most relevance to advocacy in child protection.

Children First programme: key objectives in relation to child protection advocacy

Objective 3 – ensuring that children are protected from emotional, physical, sexual abuse and neglect (significant harm).

By, for example:

- Ensuring all children using Part III services have access to complaints procedures that have been developed in consultation with looked-after children, and that these procedures involve open access to those not directly responsible for children's care.

Objective 9 – to actively involve users and carers in planning services and in tailoring individual packages of care; and to ensure that effective mechanisms are in place to handle complaints.

By, for example:
- Actively seeking and using children's views in the planning, delivery and review of services.
- Taking account of the views of children; and ensuring that the satisfaction of users is rising.
- Ensuring all looked after children have access to an independent visitor.

The Children First programme has provided a supportive context for child protection advocacy. It is now increasingly acknowledged that children and young people in vulnerable situations, at home or in foster care or in institutional settings, require independent support to ensure they can express their views. In Wales, the commitment to listening to children and young people was strengthened by the publication of the Waterhouse Tribunal's report *Lost in Care.*[5] This devastating report meticulously describes the terrible consequences of not responding to the complaints and concerns of children and young people. That the financial contribution of local authorities to the project has grown significantly over the last few years reflects a growing national recognition that children and young people need effective allies and supporters outside of formal systems and agencies:

I wouldn't have gone to those meetings because, as I said earlier, I was scared. They say that they like to listen to a child's point of view as well but I wouldn't have gone so they wouldn't have had my views and I most probably wouldn't have been taken off the [child protection] register.

[Advocates are] there to support you all the way through it. They can put it better because if you're young you don't know how to pronounce things better. They're not like social workers either because... they're more pleasant.

They won't twist your words or anything like that, like social services do.

They will help you if you've got any problems, at any time. You can still ring them up at weekends. You can leave a message on their answerphone and they'll ring you back.

In addition to Children First, independent advocacy was promoted in the Government's revised *Working Together* guidance[6] on child protection, both in relation to children's and young people's participation in child protection conferences and also in establishing effective safeguards for children living away from home.

IT'S MY LIFE: INDIVIDUAL DECISION-MAKING

UCAN helps children to make contact with social services when they feel unsafe at home; the project also advises and assists children and young people on family contact and adoption issues; and it helps children initiate court proceedings, for example, to revoke their care orders.

In the 12 months up to the end of March 2001, the advocacy project supported 106 children and young people aged between five and 21 years, to contribute to individual decision-making processes. The majority of the children and young people – 67 per cent – were living in the family home when they contacted the project.

CHILD PROTECTION MEETINGS

In most situations, the advocacy project supported children and young people to express themselves in child protection case conferences. The following quote from a young person, taken from the project's most recent annual report, underlines the importance of independent advocacy:

I'm calling [UCAN] because I want someone to help me. The Social Services are making me go home today. I ran to my auntie's because I couldn't stand it anymore. I have been trying to tell them how bad things have been for me at home, but I've been told it's the law and if my mother and father want me back I have to go. There's nothing they can do.

As well as successfully supporting children and young people to express their wishes and feelings, the project's involvement led to several child protection meetings being reconvened so that the dates, times and venues were suitable for children and young people. Throughout the past 12 months, the project also assisted children and young people through court processes, and gave advice and information on a range of matters, from family contact to leaving care entitlements.

On many occasions, project workers represented children's and young people's views because they lacked the confidence or experience to speak in formal settings themselves:

> I was about ten years old. When [my advocate] went I got a piece of paper and a pen and wrote down some paragraphs on what [the advocate] could say for me, and she read it out. [The advocate] spoke up for me because I was quite shy then. She's built up my confidence now.

> I was too scared [to go to my case conference] because I didn't know what they were going to do or say.

> There's too many people there [at meetings]. It's embarrassing. I've seen what they do. They all watch when people are speaking; all eyes are on them.

In one local authority covered by UCAN, children's and young people's participation in child protection meetings has progressed considerably over the last two years. It is now common practice for children and young people to be present in these meetings, or to be represented by an advocate if they feel unable to express their views personally. Increasingly, children and young people are also accessing advocacy outside of the formal child protection stages.

INFLUENCING LOCAL POLICY AND SERVICE DEVELOPMENT

In addition to supporting individual children and young people to be heard and taken seriously, the advocacy project facilitates their involvement in policy and service development.

In December 1998, 20 children and young people took part in a Christmas event organised by the project. They subsequently formed the 'advocacy advisory group': about 15 children and young people, between the ages of seven and 16 years, are now regularly involved in a range of activities.

The advocacy advisory group has achieved a great deal, including the production of an information pack for children and young people on social services and child protection. Members also redrafted a standard letter from social services inviting children and young people to attend child protection case conferences. They transformed a formal, unfriendly letter into a positive communication, and hope that, as a result, more children and young people will be encouraged to take part in their meetings.

Children and young people from the advisory group gave a 'makeover' to rooms used by social services for child protection conferences. They placed their paintings on the walls, and made suggestions about how the environment could be made less formal and frightening to non-professionals. Some also made an information board on advocacy. The positive impact of these developments are shown in feedback from a young person attending a case conference:[7]

> I imagined a big, dark room and a big, humungous table and loads of people. But it wasn't like that. It was a light room and there were pictures on the wall and the chairperson was nice 'cause he talked to me.

There have been formal meetings between the advisory group and police and social services to share views and ideas on how child protection services can become more sensitive to children's needs and rights. These interactions have proved useful in helping professionals to understand the impact on children and young people of social services and police intervention. For example, the following statements show how children's and young people's first taste of social work or of advocacy can shape their future relationships:

> You can come home from school and they [social services] are waiting for you.

[When I first met my advocate] she had a nice smile and was all nice and happy, not like social workers.

[My advocate] made an appointment and turned up and wasn't late. You can rely on her.

Children and young people have created promotional materials – a poster and a leaflet about advocacy – and appeared on local radio to explain the importance of listening to children and young people. They have worked with the youth theatre *Raw Talent*, who used their ideas to produce short drama sketches for work with young people, professionals and elected members.

In addition to children's and young people's direct involvement in policy and service development, project staff have regular meetings with local authorities to discuss general issues and themes around individual advocacy.

PARTICIPATION AT A NATIONAL LEVEL

The project has also successfully promoted children's and young people's ideas and experiences at a national level. Its project report, *The Last Rung of the Ladder*,[8] has been widely used by practitioners across England and Wales. Extracts from the report were included in a training pack prepared by Children's Rights Officers and Advocates for the Department of Health[9] on looked-after children's and young people's participation.

UCAN has worked with young people to plan and organise workshops on advocacy in child protection. The material, including audio tapes of young people describing their experiences of abuse and of the child protection system, has been widely disseminated. The project has also contributed to national public policy. It ensured the experiences and views of children and young people involved in child protection were reflected in The Children's Society's response to the Department of Health's consultation on parental physical punishment. Further, the project was instrumental in ensuring that young people were included in discussions with local authorities and the Welsh Assembly on how best to implement new leaving care legislation. UCAN is also taking part in a university research project on children's and young people's participation, which hopefully will contribute to national policy and practice development in this area.

The appointment of Peter Clarke, in December 2000, as the first Children's Commissioner for Wales is a further sign that children's and young people's participation rights are going to be taken seriously. The Commissioner is required by law to promote and safeguard the rights of all children and young people "ordinarily resident" in Wales. A staff team of 26 has been recruited, based in North and South Wales, to work with the Commissioner. Some will have specific responsibilities to ensure the Commissioner's office is made aware of children's and young people's concerns and priorities. UCAN is committed to supporting children and young people to forge positive links with the Commissioner's office and has already begun to build bridges by placing children's rights newsboards in all secondary schools.

PARTNERS IN CHANGE: WHAT'S IMPORTANT?

The UCAN advocacy project tells us a great deal about how services can be designed and run in partnership with children and young people. It is a non-statutory service that would cease to exist if children and young people did not use it. Advocacy itself is impossible without forging genuine partnerships with individual children and young people. So what is important?

CHILD- AND YOUNG PERSON-LED

Children and young people are in the driving seat of advocacy. They decide whether to work with advocates, they are in charge of how much information they share and they control what the advocate does. This can be an extremely positive process, especially for those who feel lost or disempowered through the child protection or care system. Advocates are not employed to make assessments of children's and young people's family backgrounds or personal circumstances, and they do not have to make professional judgements about what is in their best interests. This frees them to form relationships that are driven purely by children's and young people's own agendas and wishes. Advocacy, therefore, is a crucial way of preventing children and young people from feeling isolated and alone, providing them with skilled adults who can work at their pace to try to ensure their voices are heard and acted upon.

PARTNERSHIP WORKING

UCAN has positive relationships with its partner local authorities. This is essential if children's and young people's experiences and views are to result in wider organisational changes. Procedures have been established to enable the regular sharing of information on how systems can be further improved to promote children's and young people's rights. Over the years, the project has developed positive relationships with senior officers within its partner local authorities and it has political backing from elected members.

The project's advisory group has been invaluable in ensuring that UCAN influences practice and policy development. The group is also an important mechanism for developing the skills and knowledge of advocacy staff.

RIGHTS FRAMEWORK

UCAN works within the framework of the UNCRC and has a particular focus on children's participation rights. Its shop-front office displays posters and leaflets that positively communicate the project's commitment to children's rights, and all materials for children and young people are presented in a rights context.

Projects and services founded on a commitment to children's human rights are extremely attractive to children and young people because they do not focus on individual difficulties or failings. Instead, they stress the need for wider organisational and cultural change. They also tend to be more attuned to the concerns and priorities of children and young people, and actively seek to engage them as equal partners.

ACTION-BASED

Advocacy is much more than listening. It is about influencing decision-making and achieving positive change – for individuals and groups as well as for organisations and wider society.

Since its inception, the UCAN project has maintained a sharp focus on working with children and young people – not only to improve individual lives and circumstances but also to contribute to policy and practice development. As the project leader explains:

Children and young people have infiltrated adult processes and, through taking part, have helped to change them for the better.

The emphasis on acting on children's and young people's experiences and views has resulted in the project carrying out a range of work extending beyond individual advocacy. This has included: seminars, training and conferences for professionals working in child protection; producing publications and other materials; meetings with senior managers and elected members; workshops for young people on advocacy and the child protection system; and lobbying on national policy issues such as a pressing need for law reform on parental physical punishment.

STAFF ATTITUDES AND SKILLS

The young people I met who had personal experience of the project stressed that the advocacy workers value and respect them. They were impressed by the accessibility of the advocacy workers and by their reliability and responsiveness. They valued the knowledge and experience the workers had of social services and the child protection system. They also stressed the importance of confidentiality and workers not sharing information without their consent or knowledge. One young person added that she felt advocates respected children's right to privacy whereas "Social workers want to know every single detail."

WHAT NEXT?

The project has produced a rights pack for children and young people entering the care system, covering the Children Act 1989 and the UNCRC. Children's and young people's knowledge and use of the pack will be monitored through the childcare reviewing system. Project information sheets are circulated to all social workers in the partner local authorities, and to parents and foster carers. A consultation day on child protection is being planned for secondary school students as a follow-up to an awareness-raising event run by the project. Advocacy workers will also assist young people to prepare an audiotape of important messages for social services for professionals and elected members.

NOT ANOTHER FORM OF SOCIAL WORK

One of the project workers has considerable social work experience. She explains that conventional social work often inhibits positive communication and relationships between children, young people and professionals.

There is a tremendous difference between working as a social worker and as an advocate. My focus has changed completely. Then [as a social worker] I had to have a general picture, whereas now [as an advocate] I am looking purely at the perspective of young people... I was always unhappy with the way it was [in social work].

UCAN has pioneered children's advocacy in the child protection system. While there has been a steady growth in advocacy for looked-after children over the past ten years, developments have been slow in this particular area of social work. The young people I spoke to gave graphic descriptions of the traumatic and frightening processes involved in child protection, which shows that much work needs to be done. On a more positive note, the young people gave glowing accounts of how advocacy can help children and young people in similar situations. As one of them explained:

[Children need] just someone who can be there to help you and give you advice about anything. [Advocates] are there to help you whenever you need them. You can rely on them.

For more information about the UCAN project, please contact:

Janet Wyllie
UCAN
12 Hanbury Road
Pontypool
Torfaen
NP4 6JL

Tel: 01495 740744
E-mail: UCAN@childrenssociety.org.uk

Research in a field: the young carers' festivals

BACKGROUND

Caring for others is an everyday feature of family life. There is nothing unusual in children and adults helping and supporting each other. Founded on mutual love and respect, this can be one of the most positive aspects of family life.

Yet up to 51,000[1] children and young people across the UK have domestic and household responsibilities above and beyond the average for people their age. Young carers were first defined in law under the Carers Recognition and Services Act 1995, which states that a young carer is an under-18-year-old "who provides or intends to provide a substantial amount of care on a regular basis".

Children and young people can find themselves with exceptional caring responsibilities because one or more of their parents, siblings or other relatives has an impairment or illness, or may be coping with drug or alcohol addiction. Their responsibilities can include: practical tasks such as shopping and cleaning; physical tasks such as lifting and personal care; and they can also involve providing emotional support and care for younger siblings. When the level of caring becomes inappropriate, it can impact on young people's happiness and personal development.

THE NEEDS OF YOUNG CARERS

Since the late 1980s, there has been a wealth of research undertaken that has raised awareness of young carers and their needs, and resulted in guidance and legislation being put into place. As well as asking for support for themselves, children and young people have asserted their need to be listened to. They have asked for time out, for the chance to do normal things for people their age, and for the opportunity to meet others in the same position. They have asked for more understanding from teachers, GPs and social workers, of both their own needs and also for those they care for.

In 1995, The Children's Society published an important research report, called *Couldn't Care More*.[2] Young carers' own words were a central feature and, for many children and young people, this was their first opportunity to talk about the highs and lows of their caring responsibilities.

Couldn't Care More identified the needs and views of young carers, aged between eight and 15 years living in Hampshire, the home of The Children's Society Young Carers Initiative. Two factors led to the research being carried out. First, a service manager from Hampshire County Council Social Services Department had been working with young disabled people, and was becoming increasingly concerned that siblings' needs were not being addressed. At the same time, the pioneering work at the University of Loughborough on young carers was beginning to make an impact nationally.[3]

YOUNG CARERS IN WINCHESTER

Following the publication of *Couldn't Care More*, Hampshire County Council Social Services and North and Mid Hants Health Authority commissioned The Children's Society to establish and support a young carers' project in Winchester.

The project was extremely successful both in supporting children and young people to express their views and in offering on-going support and information. Accessible materials were produced for local young carers, including posters and leaflets. Young people from the project took part in the production of a national video for schools, called *Talking About It*,[4] about young people's mental health. A variety of events, including one at the House of Commons, gave young carers the chance to communicate powerfully their needs and experiences to local and national decision-makers.

Further, a website designed by Hampshire County Council Social Services, in partnership with young carers, won acclaim in

November 2000 when it was 'highly commended' in the national *Community Care* awards for new and innovative service to carers. On the same day, the Department of the Environment, Transport and the Regions described the site as a positive example of providing information and help to young people living in England's rural areas.

Since April 1999 the young carers' project has been independently managed, although The Children's Society remains involved through its management committee.

RESEARCH WITH FORMER YOUNG CARERS

As well as providing direct support and encouragement for children and young people, The Children's Society carried out further research and extensive practice development work at both local and national level. *On Small Shoulders,*[5] published jointly with the Open University School of Health and Social Welfare in 1999, drew on the experiences of former young carers. It was based on interviews with 25 people, mainly from the Hampshire area, and questionnaires with a further 41 people living in different parts of the country. The report describes three levels of social exclusion facing former young carers:

- deliberate self-exclusion from activities and relationships that commonly characterise childhood;
- enforced exclusion, where children and young people were prevented from seeking outside help by their parents' behaviour;
- sanctioned exclusion, where the complacency and ignorance of welfare professionals left young carers alone and isolated.

One woman reflected on her teenage years with her younger brother and her mother, who developed multiple sclerosis. She described how, despite regular visits from district nurses, she was left to do most of the physical caring. She recalled a social worker telling her to ring if anything went wrong. The absurdity of this comment struck with her:

Well it is wrong, so how can it get wronger?[6]

Another explained the consequences of being left to cope with her mother's terminal illness:

My mother was dying of cancer... they sent her home to die from hospital... The family was more or less left alone... The cost to me was enormous. I was looking after my mother and father as well. It took up all my life for two or three years.[7]

The research has had an impact on policy: in May 2000, the local inter-agency policy for supporting young carers was jointly published by Hampshire County Council, two local health authorities and The Children's Society. The document is premised on the UNCRC and stresses the right of every child to a positive and fulfilling childhood. Importantly, professionals are reminded of the absolute necessity of taking into account the views of children and young people when carrying out assessments.

CONSULTATION WITH A DIFFERENCE – THE YOUNG CARERS' FESTIVAL 2000

In partnership with the Princess Royal Trust for Carers, The Children's Society is now compiling a good practice guide (due June 2002) on working with young carers, based on the experiences and views of children and young people.

When the idea for this national publication was first discussed, project workers considered how to ensure children's and young people's involvement. They chose an unusual method, as Peter Cooper, from the YMCA Fairthorne Manor, explains:[8]

In December 1999 Jenny Frank of The Children's Society shared with me a dream of gathering together a group of young carers from all over the UK for a weekend's conference. It was estimated that the numbers could be as high as a hundred. Immediately I knew that something out of the ordinary was going to happen. As Jenny described the need for a fun weekend, with opportunities for young people to relax, meet others and record their views and needs, a clear picture of the event entered my mind. The dream was contagious.

The two organisations decided to pool their skills and resources, and less than six months later, during a sunny weekend in June 2000, over 600 children and young people descended on the YMCA at Fairthorne Manor in Hampshire.

Children and young people between the ages of 10 and 17 years came from towns and cities, as well as from isolated rural communities. Many had travelled far, arriving from Glasgow, Wakefield, Nottingham and the Isle of Man. Despite their differences, all the children and young people had one thing in common: they had left their family responsibilities behind for a few days. One of the young volunteers working at the YMCA over the festival period, herself a young carer, explained:

> We feel we are different to kids who come from 'normal' families... Then there are the deep-down feelings of guilt and anger... The first time somebody else told me about these feelings, I was amazed; somebody else feels the same – and there were going to be 600 of us together, with similar feelings and experiences. Some of us would be complete strangers, yet we would all be at ease with each other, knowing that nothing needed to be explained... and there were people to listen. I was nearly jumping out of my skin with excitement.

The event was advertised to young carers' groups across the UK and most children and young people brought their own project workers.

A FUN WAY TO CONSULT

The programme of events across the three days included supervised activities such as archery, abseiling, canoeing, boating, and the extremely popular aerial runway. There were discos in the evenings and a 'Challenge' on Sunday to which every group entered a team. A 20-minute firework display on the first evening added to the atmosphere. The whole event ran smoothly, despite first-night nerves that there wouldn't be enough tents for everyone.

The young carers' festival 2000 was organised as a consultation event. From the outset there was a commitment to weave the experiences and views of participants into the forthcoming good practice guide. Yet equally important was the need to ensure children and young people were given the chance to relax, have fun and socialise.

The consultation methods had to be participatory and fun, in order to fit in with the festival mood. Children's and young people's views were sought in several ways.

- The 'wish wall' was a central feature where festival goers could write their thoughts and feelings. At the end of the festival, helium-filled coloured balloons were released from the wall, carrying the hopes and wishes of hundreds of children and young people into the sky.
- Young reporters interviewed fellow young carers about family life, school and messages for the Government.
- The 'young carers' voice' newsroom, equipped with PCs and laptops, was a place where children and young people could take time out to send messages to the Government, as well as to write their stories and reflect on the weekend.
- Display boards around the festival site (grouped according to themes such as 'What do schools need to do to help young carers?' and 'How does your young carers project help you?') provided opportunities for impromptu thoughts and ideas.

Staff from The Children's Society and YMCA Fairthorne Manor were available throughout the festival to listen to children and young people, either individually or in groups. In addition, representatives from Hampshire Social Services were on hand to demonstrate their website and to give children and young people essential information about services and support groups.

Young carers from Hampshire, Southampton and Bournemouth designed the festival logo, used on invitations and T-shirts. They were also part of the festival planning group and were presented with framed copies of the festival invitation at the end of event.

The YMCA Fairthorne Manor produced a celebratory review document – *Young Carers' Festival Voice* in November 2000. This attractive festival report brought together a selection of children's and young people's comments and views, and featured photographs and supportive messages from politicians.

I hope you are having a great time. Young carers deserve more chances to have time to themselves, time for studies, time for fun and a break from their responsibilities.

Extract from message of support, John Hutton MP,
Minister of State for Health

The report was circulated to all participants, as well as to young carers' projects that were unable to take part. Government ministers and senior managers in local authorities and other organisations were also sent copies.

TOGETHER WE ARE STRONG

The importance of sharing time, thoughts and space with others with similar experiences cannot be overstated. Jenny Frank and Peter Cooper, the main organisers of the festival, noticed the look of sheer wonder on many of the children's and young people's faces as they stepped out of their cars and minibuses: here was a field full of children and young people just like them.

A few days earlier, these children and young people might have believed they were the only people in their school, street or neighbourhood who had to lift their mum or dad on and off the toilet. The day before, some of them were probably too embarrassed to tell their friends what life was like at home with an alcoholic parent. The week before, some of them might have had to turn down an invitation to go bowling or hang out with their mates. Yet, on this weekend, they could do as they pleased and they were in the company of 600 people, all with the same experience of caring for others. They felt valued, understood and respected.

I have been a young carer for eight years. I have never been to a festival like this and it is weird knowing that everyone around you is having similar problems... I am having a real blast. All the people are being really understanding and are just really helpful and kind.

I think that one of the best things about coming to Fairthorne Manor is all the people you meet. It's a great thing that you can talk to people that are in the same predicament as you are.

I thought I was the only person in the whole world who had to look after their mum but I'm not. I'm really happy I came.

There was huge media interest in the festival, which was reported by local and national television. On the first day of the festival, BBC Breakfast News broadcast a typical day in the life of a young carer. A film crew from Carlton TV was on site gathering footage for a programme on young carers. There was also extensive radio coverage, including on *The World Tonight* and BBC World Service, and several newspapers positively reported the event.

2001 WAS BIGGER AND BETTER

No sooner had the tents and canoes been packed away than a decision was made to run another young carers' festival in 2001, in response to overwhelming requests from young people.

It's a good idea because you can come here to have fun and not worry so much. I would come again if they hold another one!

At the end of June 2001, over 1,200 children and young people took part in the second young carers' festival. This time, children and young people from several UK projects were part of the planning group, and bursaries were available to help with travel costs.

PLANNING AHEAD

The planning group included young people from Glasgow, Bradford, London, Kent and Worcester, as well as Hampshire and Southampton. They again designed the logo and invitations, and wrote to some television personalities and their favourite singers. An invitation was also sent to the Prime Minister.

During a planning weekend, young people designed a stage set and created a music video that opened the festival and was played throughout the event. They met the catering manager for the event to give advice on food and refreshments. The planning group also prepared a news bulletin about their preparatory weekend and sent it to all the projects taking part in the festival. A focus group was held to design a questionnaire, with the group considering the following question: "What actions need to be taken in order to improve services for you and your families?" The young people produced a long list of answers that were fed into the Priority Search®⁹ computer research programme, which created a questionnaire. This was then sent to all children and young people attending the festival. The top ten priorities from their answers were translated into open questions to enable qualitative consultation during the festival. This generated over 200 responses that will be incorporated into the forthcoming good practice guide on young carers.

A *FIELD OF INTERACTIVE FUN*
Festival 2001 had zones for different activities, including circus skills and rap workshops, a coffee shop, a 'music fringe tent' and a chill-out area. The consultation area evolved from the first year into the Voice Zone with many additional interactive consultation activities, including the use of Priority Search, roving reporters and a cartoon and comic strip workshop. The information generated was channelled through the onsite newsroom, with children and young people writing and editing two festival bulletins. The second bulletin was distributed hot off the photocopier to all the children and young people as they left, enabling them to have something to show their family and friends when they got home. They could also use the bulletin to promote their work locally.

Film footage was also taken over the weekend, now produced on CD-Rom and video cassette for all projects. Media coverage was again high, with *Blue Peter* filming the whole weekend for a documentary, to be screened in June 2002.

A *FORCE FOR CHANGE*
The festival as a force for change, as well as a field of fun, was emphasised by the presentations made by some of the young carers to a range of decision-makers, including representatives from the Children and Young People's Unit and the Department of Health.

Four young carers took the hopes and wishes of festival participants to the All-party Parliamentary Group for Children in July 2001. They spoke with authority and conviction, and gave many examples of the kinds of practical changes that need to happen to ensure young carers and their families receive appropriate support.

So energised was the All-party Parliamentary Group that they immediately took steps to engage relevant Government departments to promote better co-ordination and approaches to meeting the needs of young carers and their families. The joint chairs of the All-party Group invited the four young people to return in a year's time to hear what progress has been made.

PARTNERS IN CHANGE: WHAT'S IMPORTANT?

Several factors contributed to the success of both these young carers' festivals.

First, the partnership between The Children's Society and the YMCA Fairthorne Manor proved extremely positive. Both organisations share a commitment to children's rights and participation. Staff have the skills required – including administration, logistics, running group activities, and consultation and participation methods (on a large scale) – for an event of this kind. Detailed planning for 2001 began the previous autumn, with specific tasks delegated within a partnership agreement.

Second, the involvement of young people in the festival planning group was important, although their role was restricted in the first year, due to a lack of time and resources. Their greater participation in planning the 2001 festival significantly enhanced the range and relevance of activities, and the means and effectiveness of the consultation.

A clear lesson is that open access consultation does work. The children and young people who decided to contribute their ideas and experiences did so through choice. The method that was particularly successful was peer journalism, with use of tape recorders, digital cameras and video. The computer bank in the 'news room' was also popular. As one reporter put it:

I really enjoyed hearing other people's views.

Finally, the festival would have been nothing without the children and young people who took part. Jenny Frank, co-ordinator of the Young Carers Initiative, describes an "amazing atmosphere" characterised by a huge amount of caring and sharing.

MORE THAN LISTENING

Too often organisations invest a huge amount of time and resources into one-off consultation events but never get round to considering children's and young people's ideas and suggestions seriously. Everyone has an enjoyable, uplifting time but nothing much changes for children and young people.

The Children's Society has learned that to ensure that large-scale events are truly consultative and participative, an enormous amount of time and energy is needed. YMCA Fairthorne Manor brought their vision and organisational expertise to the events, and support from many Children's Society colleagues ensured the festivals were successful. Local volunteers were recruited to help with preparations for the first festival and to provide crucial support at the event. The incredible amount of time and effort required in arranging and running the festivals has paid off, resulting in much positive action for young carers, both at a local and a national level.

The media coverage for both festivals increased awareness among many local authorities and, as a result, directly benefited some of the projects that attended. Following the festival in 2001, the messages were taken to the heart of Government via the All-party Parliamentary Group for Children. Further, information obtained from both festivals has informed the content of the national good practice guide, which The Children's Society is publishing with the Princess Royal Trust for Carers.

With funding from the Department of Health, The Children's Society has now developed a national initiative across England to support young carers to directly influence practice and policy development. The festival consultation has given them a wealth of information on both the lives of young carers and what kinds of methods can excite and engage children and young people.

The young carers' festivals prove that large-scale consultation can be fun, meaningful and effective for children and young people. Jenny Frank's dream of bringing together young carers from all over the UK to have fun and share their stories came true because of the effort, determination and shared vision of two children's organisations and young people working together. Who knows what future years will bring?

For more information about the young carers festivals, please contact:

Jenny Frank
Young Carers Initiative
Youngs Yard
Finches Lane
Twyford
Nr Winchester
SO21 1NN

Tel: 01962 711511
E-mail: young-carers-initiative@childrenssociety.org.uk

Ask Us! Young disabled people get active

BACKGROUND

In 1997 a poster appeared on a noticeboard in Chris Martin's school, a mainstream secondary in the West Midlands with support for young disabled people. The poster said that The Children's Society was setting up a video club for young disabled students. Chris was interested and decided to join, believing it would be a safe place where "people wouldn't be nasty or discriminating".[1] He was 12 years old at the time.

The club met on a Monday immediately after school. The timing was convenient for the young people and their parents because it saved having to make travel arrangements. Food was provided during the first half-hour of the meeting.

When Chris went to his first meeting, he was expecting to be shown videos. He was surprised when the adult facilitators explained that this was a chance to make a video, rather than watch someone else's.

Staff from The Children's Society Solihull project encouraged the seven club members to talk about their experiences of being young and disabled. This was the first chance the students had ever had to share their experiences of prejudice and discrimination. It also gave them the opportunity to talk about their hopes and aspirations. Chris describes one young person saying that discussions about the future didn't apply to him because he was going to die in a few years. This had a profound effect on Chris who had never before heard about the challenges facing other young disabled people.

The idea for and success of the video club can largely be attributed to Maureen Murray, who was then managing a short-term residential unit for young disabled people. Maureen had worked for The Children's Society for over 20 years, and was committed to helping young disabled people to express their views and be taken seriously. She decided to set up the video club because many of the young people using short-term care were students at the school. Maureen had heard many negative stories over the years about how disabled students were treated and felt it was important to try to address these difficulties from within the school.

In order to galvanise support for the group among teachers and parents, Maureen met with the head of the school's resource unit for young people with a physical impairment, and had meetings with the headteacher and the rest of the teaching staff. Letters were also sent to the parents or carers of disabled students. Parents saw the whole concept of the group as positive – for many it was the first invitation their daughter or son had received to join a social group – while teaching staff had reservations but did not sabotage the group in any way.

'TAKING DOWN THE WALL' THROUGH DRAMA

The group met for a year, during which time it expanded to include young people from the school who had specific learning impairments. Notes were taken at each session. At the end of the year, Maureen used these notes to write a script for a play and video about the challenges and discrimination facing young disabled people.

Group members, other young people, volunteers and some parents performed the play to an invited audience of 300 people at Solihull Library Theatre in 1998. There were a further 100 people on the waiting list. The play focused on the difference between integration and inclusion. As Chris explains, just opening the school gates to young disabled people is not enough:

You could be sitting in a class but sitting on your own.

The audience included professionals, such as teachers and social workers, as well as those working in leisure services, and journalists from regional and local newspapers. A questionnaire was circulated before and after the play to assess whether there had been any immediate changes in understanding among the audience.

An artificial wall was built in the theatre: at the end of the play everyone was given one of the miniature bricks to take home, which had been specially made for the project by a local museum. There was a label on the inside of the brick, with the words "We took down the wall."

Being involved in the play strengthened Chris' commitment to disability equality:

> That was the point that I knew I wanted to go on. When I heard that people had been crying I knew I could make a difference.

Another group member commented afterwards:

> This is the best day of my life; this has changed my life.[2]

THE SPEAK UP, SPEAK OUT GROUP

After the play, the group decided to continue meeting but they reformed themselves as the Speak Up, Speak Out group. They made a deliberate decision to move from being a club with a social focus, to a group with a more political agenda:

> We wanted to get things changed.

Their first major project was to prepare materials on buddying for use in schools. The theme was on respecting and valuing difference, and the materials were titled *Learning Together*. Group members presented their work to a large group of teachers, health workers, council members and social services staff in July 1999. Professionals were asked to complete questionnaires before and after the group's presentation to assess their own attitudes towards inclusion and participation.

FROM SMALL SEEDS ... THE QUALITY PROTECTS PROGRAMME

With this experience and energy, it is no surprise that young people from the Speak Up, Speak Out group were keen to get involved during 2000–2001 in a national consultation involving six Children's Society projects in England, as part of the Government's Quality Protects programme.

The idea of using a multimedia approach to this national consultation came from Lynette Partington, who worked at the Transitions project in Southport and is now a freelance consultant. Lynette wanted to establish a consultation project that was genuinely inclusive and meaningful to disabled children and young people. Together with other colleagues in The Children's Society, Lynette saw that the Quality Protects programme presented a unique opportunity for young disabled people to influence a national Government initiative.

Quality Protects programme: the Government's objectives for children's social services

The Government has set 11 objectives for children's social services. All of these apply to young disabled people. However, two are of particular concern:

Objective 6 – Meeting the Needs of Disabled Children and their Families

To ensure that children with specific social needs arising out of disability or a health condition are living in families or other appropriate settings in the community where their assessed needs are adequately met and reviewed.

By:

- making sure that local authorities and the health service have a complete picture of the numbers and circumstances of disabled children in their area;
- providing more and better family support to help disabled children and their families live ordinary lives;

- helping more disabled and non-disabled children use the same play and leisure services;
- giving children and parents information about the services which might help them.

Objective 8 – Actively Involving Users and Carers

To actively involve users and carers in planning services and in tailoring individual packages of care; and to ensure effective mechanisms are in place to handle complaints.

By:

- actively involving children and families in planning and reviewing the services they use, and in the decisions which affect them;
- ensuring that children in care have trusted people to whom they can speak and who will speak on their behalf to local authorities and to others;
- showing that children and families are becoming more satisfied with services.

The Disabled Children National Reference Group is one of several expert groups set up by the Department of Health to advise the five-year Quality Protects programme. From the outset, the group, chaired by the Joseph Rowntree Foundation, was determined to obtain and take seriously the views and experiences of children and young people across England.

With additional funding from the Joseph Rowntree Foundation, The Children's Society supported over 200 young disabled people to share their ideas on how the Government's Quality Protects programme can support them and their families. The England-wide consultation with 4- to 24-year-olds had five core questions:

Quality Protects programme: national consultation with young disabled people

Core questions

- What do you enjoy doing in your spare time?
- What would you like to do more of?
- What are your experiences of consultation?
- What are your experiences of participation in services?
- What do you understand by inclusion?

MULTIMEDIA CONSULTATIONS

The Speak Up, Speak Out group picked up the challenge and continued to meet on an informal basis, with members carrying out three different multimedia consultations. Three young women – Catherine, Beki and Louise – undertook research on how useful and inclusive telephone helplines are to young disabled people. Other members invested their time and energy into trying to get their local council to make playgrounds and play spaces accessible to young wheelchair users. Chris and his 16-year-old friend Marc expanded their learning by using animation to express their views and ideas. They received technical support and advice from professional filmmakers at the IMAX cinema in London. Chris describes these separate projects as "little things for a big goal".

The Disabled Bit, the title of the animation produced by Chris and Marc, depicts two employees talking about the arrival of their new manager. They have been told to add the inclusion of disabled people to their meeting agenda. They call this 'the disabled bit'. However, they soon become side-tracked and start imagining what their new manager is like. They note he has a first class degree, a sports car and is very attractive to women. They jokingly compare this with the fate of disabled people. The two employees expose their deep ignorance and prejudices while the audience is shown that the new manager is a wheelchair user. The manager hears the ridiculous ramblings of his employees through the intercom system. The animation ends with him entering the room smiling, met by his two red-faced employees.

All of the children's and young people's views and messages from the Ask Us! consultation process were used to produce six PowerPoint presentations on CDs, each focusing on different areas of exclusion, including access to play and leisure opportunities, educational experiences, and relationships with friends and families. As well as using graphics, cartoons and video, three of the groups wrote and performed songs to communicate their ideas and experiences. In addition, Lynette Partington compiled a summary CD,[2] aimed at key people in local authorities with responsibility to take forward Quality Protects locally.[3]

The children's and young people's pioneering work was launched at a celebration event, called Ask Us! in Birmingham in April 2001.

Children and young people ran workshops where they described their work, and gave advice on lessons learned. Over 200 people took part in the conference, including representatives from both the Department of Health and the Joseph Rowntree Foundation. The speaker from the Department of Health promised to share the powerful messages of children's and young people's exclusion with colleagues across Government departments, especially within the Department for Education and Skills. Ian Sparks, the chief executive of The Children's Society, called for radical change in the way young disabled people are treated:

> We can't go on like this. These children and young people are part of this world. There should be one world together, for all of us.

There are major benefits to using multimedia to support young disabled people to express their views and ideas. Many young disabled people are familiar and skilled at using computers and other technical equipment. This approach allows young disabled people to make presentations and appear on television without personal assistants or adult facilitators. Young people involved in Ask Us! have presented their work to local and national Government, and to a number of conferences for professionals working with children and young people. Using multimedia allows young people to work at a pace that suits them, working out what they want to say, how they want to say it, and to whom. Mistakes can easily be rectified and there are no pressures associated with speaking at conferences or in public meetings.

Having recognised the value and potential impact of this type of approach – in effecting change in organisations and in professional practice and promoting the personal empowerment of the young people involved – the Department of Health has funded the consultation into a second year. This time a CD will also be produced on the consultation process, as well as on the messages and evidence from children and young people.

THE CHALLENGE OF SOCIAL INCLUSION

Young disabled people face many forms of social exclusion – within their own families, throughout the education system, in their local communities, within national and local politics, and in the media. Article 23 of the UNCRC stresses their right to "social integration" and "active participation in the community". Yet young disabled people have to struggle to achieve the same level of respect and inclusion as their non-disabled contemporaries.

The day-to-day challenges facing disabled people are commonly seen as arising from personal deficiencies rather than as a consequence of a disabling society that fails to acknowledge or celebrate difference. Medical and welfare professionals invest huge amounts of resources into trying to cure or rehabilitate children and young people who they see as abnormal. Special schools that perpetuate segregation and social exclusion are still defended, and many charities have been slow to abandon stereotypical images of young disabled people. Inevitably, then, any initiative to further the social inclusion of young disabled people must counter their negative experiences, and support them to increase their aspirations and expectations from life.

A CATALYST FOR POSITIVE CHANGE

Being involved in the video club and the Ask Us! consultation has transformed Chris. He explains:

> When I was a little boy I was really shy and I wouldn't want to speak out.

Now he is determined to make full use of his talents and experiences to ensure positive changes for disabled people. He still faces prejudice: ironically, on the day he went to London with his friend Marc to an animation workshop, where they produced the skit on disability inequality, they stopped off for breakfast at a motorway service station. A waitress offered Chris and Marc hats and crayons, even though they were 15 and 16 years old. A similar thing happened on their return journey, when a waitress held up crayons at the car window as she fetched food and drinks.

Chris is extremely positive about Maureen Murray's role in helping him to express himself and have his views taken seriously:

> *When I first met Maureen I thought she was really nice and unlike other people. Maureen was different. She knew, I don't know why she just seems to know. She's not patronising like other people. She's really helped me to change as a person and to express my views.*

Clearly the respectful relationships between young people and this member of staff was a critical factor in the success of the group. Chris pointed out the subtleties of a disabling society when he explained the tendency of adults to respond excessively to day-to-day achievements:

> *You may subconsciously see young people as equals but then you over-praise them.*

CHALLENGING DISCRIMINATORY BEHAVIOUR AND ATTITUDES

Most of the time the group tried to use positive methods to raise awareness and encourage people to see, think and act differently. However, there have been one or two times where they have had to challenge behaviour and attitudes bluntly. One example was when Chris's school reported on the play that was performed at the Solihull Library Theatre. The teacher who wrote the piece got the date, time, venue and title wrong. Naturally, the group was offended, and one of the young women decided to write a letter of complaint. This resulted in the group meeting the headteacher.

There are other incidents that the group decided not to tackle, such as when the headteacher asked the group to choose plants for the school garden. Chris explains:

> *We're trying to get away from being patronised. We want to be included in the school curriculum rather than included tokenistically.*

Another time, a teacher sat in the room where the social club was meeting; when politely asked to leave the room, she replied: "Oh I don't mind you being here, just carry on." Of course the content of the group's performances was also challenging. Chris remembers a group member countering ignorance about disabled people when "he actually had the guts to say 'yes, we do have sex too'".

WORKING THROUGH DIFFICULTIES

As the young people's confidence and awareness grew so too did their dissatisfaction with various aspects of their school life. At one stage, this led to Speak Up, Speak Out members challenging the work of the group facilitators. They were disheartened by the growing gap between their expectations and the lack of positive impact the group was having in their school. For example, during one session, members had a long discussion about their continuing experiences in school of being bullied and treated differently by their peers. They observed that teaching staff did not seem to have the skills or commitment to intervene positively. Their impression was that teachers were very good at teaching subjects but were not so good at dealing with discrimination and helping young people work together well.

The group also went through a period when members complained that meetings could be boring, especially when they lacked structure or involved, for example, having to work through agreeing scripts for a forthcoming presentation or speech. On occasion young people asked the adult facilitators to complete such tasks, commenting that they had already been through the work and found it too frustrating to repeat. These types of situations were resolved by the facilitators positively reminding group members of the aims of the group and supporting their desire for more social time and extended breaks. Meetings also proved to be much more productive when practical tasks were involved, such as making T-shirts, badges and banners for a forthcoming event.

SHORT-TERM NEEDS VERSUS LONG-TERM VISION

The types of concerns articulated by Speak Up, Speak Out members are common in most groups and organisations that are established to effect change. The young people in the group were passionately committed to changing their school and wider society, but several months on they had not seen any real progress.

That the group questioned their effectiveness as a change-agent at the same time as proposing that their meetings should include more social time may seem contradictory. However, it is another crucial factor in ensuring the long-term survival of groups and organisations. Individual participants have to feel they are getting something out of their involvement, and friendships and fun are extremely important in giving meaning to a group whose goals are so wide-ranging and long-term.

For some members of the Speak Up, Speak Out group this was their only opportunity to spend time with their peers beyond the school gates. Being part of a group whose purpose and activities are not adult-led continues to be rare for most children and young people. An environment where adults support rather than control gives children and young people freedom to make real choices about how they use their time. Inevitably this may at times result in the group steering off course, or changing its priorities.

PARTNERS IN CHANGE: WHAT'S IMPORTANT?

There are many people and processes involved in The Children's Society's pioneering work with young disabled people. However, several factors stand out as significant ingredients in achieving social change for and with disabled children and young people.

First, the organisation understands that the enormous challenges faced by disabled people are because of society, not individual incapacity. They have rejected the medical model of disability, where disabled people are perceived and treated as ill or sick, in favour of the social model, which stresses that it is society that must change.

Second, adults working with young disabled people in The Children's Society recognise that they have as much to learn from children and young people as they have to give. They do not see or treat children and young people as empty vessels. They celebrate each child's and young person's unique contribution and see their role as being to enable children and young people to take as much control of their lives as possible.

Third, children and young people have been enabled to choose their own working practices and communication methods. Young disabled people have not been restricted by having to use professional forms of communication, such as reports and speeches at conferences (although they have also done this). They have been supported to express their ideas and views in familiar and creative ways at a pace that suits them.

Fourth, the organisation has supported the personal growth and development of children and young people. Young disabled people receive very few public messages about their own personal worth, or about the positive role of disabled people in society. Like their non-disabled peers, they are unlikely to learn about children's human rights within the education system, or to be routinely encouraged to contribute to decision-making processes. They may have internalised negative attitudes that prevail in society and adjusted their hopes and aspirations accordingly. The role of adults within organisations committed to social justice can be crucial in supporting children and young people to realise their dreams, and positively claim their human rights. As Maureen Murray explains:

You've got to work hard all the time to create opportunities for them to be heard.

Finally, there has been a growing commitment not only to supporting young disabled people to make changes to the external world but also to making changes within The Children's Society. For example, Chris and other young people have written (and been paid for) The Children's Society's policy on television viewing in residential units. As a young person who helped carry out the Quality Protects research concluded:

I enjoyed for once being on the other side of the fence...and I enjoy making a difference to other young people's lives.[3]

For more information about the Speak Up, Speak Out group, please contact:

Maureen Murray
St. Christopher's Shared Care
625 Warwick Road
Solihull
B91 1AP

Tel: 0121 709 2610
E-mail: maureen.murray@childrenssociety.org.uk

For more information about the Ask Us! national consultation for Quality Protects, please contact:

Margaret Hart
8 Vine Street
Kersal
Salford
Manchester
M7 3PG

Tel: 0161 792 8885
E-mail: margaret.hart@childrenssociety.org.uk

Small voices count too: The Children's Society under-eights development project

BACKGROUND

In 1998, The Children's Society was approached by a middle manager of a London social services department. He wanted the local authority's under-eights review to be carried out from a children's rights perspective, and felt The Children's Society would be ideal for the task.

Section 19 of the Children Act 1989 requires local authorities in England and Wales to review the provision of daycare and childminding services for under-eights every three years. The reviews should be carried out jointly by social services and local education authorities.

The local authority invested a considerable amount of money into this three-year consultation project. Their contribution was matched by The Children's Society. The aims of the consultation project were:

- to ensure that the child's perspective is represented in the Section 19 review and used to inform the planning and development processes within the borough;
- to devise effective methods of consultation to ascertain the experiences children under eight have of the services that affect them;
- to have consulted a minimum of 200 children, incorporating children from different age and ethnic minority groups, with a

disability or special educational needs and from different areas of the borough;
- to demonstrate that even very young children are capable of informing the local authority's planning and development strategies.

HOW THE CONSULTATION WAS CONDUCTED

Four sessional workers were recruited to carry out the consultations with children and parents. They all had positive links with diverse local communities, including with religious groups. Between them, the workers spoke five languages, which proved to be an incredible asset.

Two methods were used to elicit children's views and feelings: observation and activities. Before starting any of their work with children, the project workers were given advice and training from their manager.

Under-eights review: consulting very young children

Principles
These principles apply to all children regardless of their race, gender or ability.
- No child is considered too young to indicate what matters to them.
- Children's learning is active and as such they can learn to participate if given the opportunity to do so.
- Children have a right to express their views and to be listened to.
- Children's feelings are as strong and valid as those of adults.
- The work is to be child-centred and child led at all times.

Practice guidelines
Project workers were expected to:
- Earn children's trust by working with them as equals.
- Use the medium of play at all times.
- Actively listen to children and not interpret what they say.
- Always use tools that can capture children's imagination.

- Avoid structured question-and-answer sessions.
- Ensure that each consultation process has a structure.
- Ensure that each consultation process does not disrupt the group.
- Thank children for their participation.
- Dress appropriately – wear practical loose clothing that is OK to get messy.

OBSERVATIONS

Wherever possible, children were observed in their daycare setting, after-school club or activity session before being consulted. Observations took three forms:

- **Objective observer** – where workers recorded children's movements and choices but had no personal interaction with children.
- **Participant observer** – where workers joined in as equal playmates.
- **Observer as a curiosity** – where workers sat apart from children, watching and writing, provoking children's curiosity and subsequent dialogue and conversation.

ACTIVITIES

These were designed around children's preferences and included group brainstorming sessions, as well as artwork, video-making and photography. Children's views and ideas were obtained through one-to-one sessions as well as through small group work. Verbatim notes were taken of all consultation sessions with children. A total of 438 children were consulted during the life of the project, in 20 different settings. Not all children were aged under eight: in mixed-age settings, such as summer playschemes, there were some older children who wanted to take part in the consultation activities. The project workers did not want to exclude them from the sessions so their views and experiences were gathered too.

ENGAGING PARENTS

After each consultation session, project workers met with parents or carers to share children's views 'and ideas and to obtain further information. In all, the project informed and consulted 380 parents/ carers (327 females, 53 males).

WHAT YOUNG CHILDREN WANTED

Responses from children were grouped according to their different age groups. Project workers concluded that children between the age of 18 months and three years were mostly concerned with their families, play and the weather. Three- to five-year-olds tended to focus on families, parks and going out, while five- to seven-year-olds generally focused on parks and friends. Children from the age of seven upwards concentrated on their friends, the environment and going out.

Throughout the consultation, children made many suggestions as to how their lives and environments could be improved. The most common suggestions were:

- less dog mess;
- more play equipment;
- more safe places to meet friends;
- less vandalism and pollution;
- better toilet facilities in public settings, such as nurseries and primary schools;
- less smoking;
- to be listened to;
- less bullying.

WHAT YOUNG CHILDREN GOT

The Children's Society believes that the local authority has not seriously considered any of the messages from young children involved in the consultation. The children who took part have received no feedback from any of the statutory bodies that commissioned the Section 19 review. Two years after completing the review, The Children's Society has still not received any formal feedback about how children's views and wishes have informed policy and service development.

Further, aside from the consultation sessions, and one meeting between senior Conservative politicians and young children (see below), the project was unable to offer children any opportunities to share their experiences and ideas or to develop their decision-making skills.

PARTNERS IN CHANGE: WHAT WENT WRONG?

The project leader identified several factors that she believes contributed to the findings from the consultation not being taken seriously.

LACK OF SERIOUS ENGAGEMENT FROM THE OUTSET

From the beginning the project leader felt that the under-eights review was not a priority for the local authority. The steering group failed to meet regularly, and there was no monitoring of how well the project was meeting its objectives by either the local authority or the health authority.

This review was not part of a systematic process to improve policies and services for children. It did not fit anywhere structurally and there was not a single named officer (or elected member) who had responsibility for seeing the project through to the end. In this sense, the project did no more than ensure the local authority carried out its basic statutory duty to review services. As a reflection of the lack of engagement with the process or the messages, hundreds of hours of children's time and several collages, videos, paintings, banners and recorded discussions were reduced to a five-page summary report for a council meeting. No other outlet was given for children's ideas and contributions to be aired or celebrated.

Partnerships are a two-way process and the difficult issues described above raise questions about both the local authority's lack of engagement and the capacity of The Children's Society to grapple with and resolve these problems. If it was known at an early stage that the local authority was not committed to the project, and that it was unlikely therefore to act on any of the results, would it not have been better to stop the consultation and renegotiate the terms of the project?

KEY STAKEHOLDER LEAVES POST

The manager who initially approached The Children's Society, and subsequently commissioned the work, moved from his post for six months shortly after the project began. This left the project without its principal ally at a critical stage of its development.

The problem of losing key allies is a perennial one in children's rights and participatory work. The difficulties of this project are a salutary reminder of the need to engender broad support: within a local authority, this must include elected members who can be very supportive in spearheading and supporting wider organisational change.

POLITICAL SENSITIVITIES

Some of the project's activities were very sensitive politically. For example, its work with a group of six- to ten-year-olds, all from minority ethnic communities, led to a meeting with the then leader of the Conservative Party. The children were deeply concerned about the lack of play provision in their local area and talked openly about racism in the education system. They asked if the project could help them meet someone powerful who could listen to their views and make the changes they were suggesting.

The children discussed the merits of meeting the Prime Minister but opted for the leader of the Opposition as they believed he had more credibility; one of the children also had a positive association with the Conservative Party. The Children's Society subsequently arranged a visit to the project by the leader of the Opposition. The project leader acknowledges that the organisation made a political error in not notifying the local Labour MP (also a Minister of State) of the visit. This one event, arranged entirely at the request of the children concerned, seriously impeded the project's credibility, and support from key people within the borough subsequently withered. There was a prevailing assumption that the children were incapable of making such a suggestion without undue influence or coercion from the project. However, it is understandable that the local politician was unhappy about not being informed: aside from the potential political ramifications of such a visit, being notified in advance would also have been courteous.

ORGANISATIONAL DIFFICULTY

There were four different social services directors in the 12-month period of this project. The chief executive of the council also took early retirement. This state of organisational flux inevitably affected the project's capacity to learn from and respond to children's experiences and views.

Although the rate of change at senior manager level was unusually high in this local authority, organisational change is a common feature of local authorities. While lack of stability can seriously impede positive developments, it can also provide fertile ground for innovative ideas and proposals to be taken up by new people with fresh hopes and ideas for their organisation.

ATTITUDES TOWARDS YOUNG CHILDREN

Throughout the consultation period, project workers heard many negative comments from parents and professionals about consulting young children. These adults generally underestimated the capacity of young children and did not accept that society's youngest citizens have a right to be listened to and taken seriously.

It is a sad reality that none of the 438 children who were consulted for the under-eights review is likely to make their way to decision-makers to ask them to respond to their ideas and experiences. The powerlessness and invisibility of young children makes them very easy to dismiss or ignore.

A major way of tackling negative attitudes towards consulting and including young children in decision-making is to demonstrate practically the benefits of their involvement – for them as individuals, but also for the effectiveness of services and organisations that set out to meet their needs. Unfortunately, this particular project did not go beyond gathering information; therefore, there were no concrete examples of the benefits of listening to young children. However, information sheets, practice guidelines, seminars and other learning events for those working with young children could have drawn together positive examples from other participatory projects and initiatives. They could have had a positive impact on policy makers and senior managers, perhaps addressing some of the problems outlined above.

WHAT NEXT?

The Children's Society has learned an enormous amount from carrying out this under-eights review.[1] There are all the lessons, already described, about the need to establish and preserve the positive interest and commitment of key stakeholders. There are also other matters related to the nature and extent of participation for very young children.

WHO SHOULD CONDUCT THE RESEARCH?

There is a growing belief among those working with very young children that effective consultation and participation can only be meaningful to very young children if people they know, and have relationships with, facilitate it. The project leader now shares this view.

A major problem with researchers or other professionals 'jumping' in and out is that they are not personally in a position to effect the changes that children propose. They may bring impartiality and expertise in encouraging children to express their views but they are often not the most suitable people to be hearing the important things children say. This is particularly pertinent with young children because they are much more likely to request changes in their immediate environments, or raise issues that need to be addressed by their parents or carers. For example, several of the consultation sessions were held during a time when there was repeated television coverage of political unrest in the Middle East. As one young child stated:

There is going to be a war and I am going to be in it.

A positive response to this child's statement would be for the adults who are close to him to initiate discussions about where in the world there is fighting and war, and reassure him that he lives in a relatively safe country. The adults who carried out the consultation could have tried to reassure him but it would have been far more appropriate for people who know him to address his anxieties.

Even very experienced researchers can have problems conveying the richness of young children's communications when they come to writing their reports. However, if adults who know and live or work with children hear their ideas and feelings first-hand this can have more impact. It also gives them the opportunity to ask more questions. For example, as one child in the consultation said:

I like school but only 50 per cent of the time.

Someone who knew this child, and was trusted by her, would perhaps be more able to discover what lies behind this statement and if anything could be done about it.

If it is only ever strangers who ask children their views and feelings, children might get the impression that their immediate carers are not interested in their ideas. They also rarely get the chance to have follow-up conversations or ask questions about what is being done with their suggestions. Importantly, the adults who normally work or live with them may not get the opportunity to develop participative environments. Respecting young children, and treating what they say and feel seriously, should not be seen as a specialist occupation, reserved only for the very skilled or experienced.

The benefits of engaging adults close to children to elicit their feelings and wishes have long been acknowledged in relation to children and young people with learning impairments. Here it is absolutely critical that the adults carrying out the consultation, or promoting participation, know the child or young person well and can communicate with them. There is too much risk of misinterpretation, unless the person carrying out the research or consultation is able to invest the necessary time into getting to know the child or young person. The same principle applies to babies and toddlers, especially for those who are pre-language: it is impossible to understand fully what they are communicating without knowing them properly.

MOVING ON

Based on lessons learned from the under-eights review, the project leader has been supporting other Children's Society projects to develop effective methods that ensure young children are involved and listened to as part of their everyday experience. For example, in conjunction with the University of East London, the project leader is running three-day training workshops for those working with, or planning and managing services for, children aged 0–5, to equip them with the skills and knowledge to effectively listen to and involve very young children. In Cornwall, Children's Society project workers have been supported by the project leader to deliver training to Sure Start practitioners and managers on listening to and involving very young children as they adapt to their new nursery.

The Children's Society recently worked with colleagues from Save the Children to try to ensure the Greater London Authority (GLA) treats the views and ideas of some of its youngest citizens seriously.

The two organisations supported nursery staff across London to consult 32 young children they were working with, aged between two and five years. The report from the consultation, *London On Your Doorstep*,[2] has been carefully prepared so that children's ideas and views about living in London are translated into strategic proposals that staff at the GLA can easily relate to and use. Here lies another lesson: professionals carrying out consultations need to make it as easy as possible for organisations to learn from and respond to children. Large organisations and busy politicians rarely set aside time to decipher messages and meaning meticulously from consultation reports. That is why it is crucial to invest just as much care and attention in the way information is presented as to how it is gathered. Responding positively to the London consultation, the deputy mayor of the GLA, Nicky Gavron, stated:

> … *given the right encouragement even the youngest children have plenty to say about their experiences of London and how we could improve their lives.*

This is the first positive step towards opening up decision-making processes in London to very young children. No doubt it will be a long journey, but let's hope the 32 young children will hear very soon what the GLA intends to do with their advice.

For more information about The Children's Society work on consultation with very young children, please contact:

Julie McLarnon or Simon Hepburn
Early Years Project
91–93 Queen's Road
Peckham
London
SE15 2EZ

Tel: 020 7639 1466
E-mail: julie.mclarnon@childrenssociety.org.uk
simon.hepburn@childrenssociety.org.uk

Citizens Now: the Liverpool Bureau for Children and Young People

BACKGROUND

The Toxteth[1] riots in July 1981 marked the beginning of The Children's Society's involvement in an area facing severe social and economic disadvantage. At that time, youth employment in the area known as Liverpool 8 stood at 60 per cent: careers officers had only 12 vacancies for all of the city's school leavers in the summer of 1981.

A local vicar contacted The Children's Society for support in the aftermath of the riots, which led to a range of activities including the establishment of a credit union, a youth centre and support for parents of young children. The Lodge Lane Community Project, established by The Children's Society in 1985, initially offered these types of family services but gradually turned its attention to the particular difficulties facing children and young people. This development mirrored wider changes within The Children's Society, which was beginning to refocus itself as a social justice organisation for children.

THE CHILDREN'S RESEARCH GROUP

The journey towards a bureau for children and young people has its roots in research commissioned by the South West Toxteth Liaison Committee, comprising councillors, local authority employees and representatives from voluntary organisations. The Committee sought to identify the needs of children in the Liverpool 8 area. This led to a number of organisations, including The Children's Society, joining together to form the Liverpool 8 Children's Research Group in January 1993.

CHILDREN'S PRIORITIES AND CONCERNS

A pilot survey was carried out in 1993 with 129 children from two local schools, aged between seven and 11 years. A more detailed programme followed in 1996, involving over 1,000 children from ten different schools. The researchers used a Priority Search questionnaire, as well as drama and poetry workshops and neighbourhood walks. Children from one school also kept diaries.

The Children's Research Group wanted the process to be as participative and empowering for children as possible. That is why they chose the Priority Search method, which allows participants to set their own agendas. Four researchers based at the Granby Management and Development Agency carried out the research. Significantly, the researchers were local people, and all had a personal investment in achieving positive change within the Liverpool 8 area. Focus groups were held in ten different schools; six of these were in the heart of the Liverpool 8 area, two were on the periphery and a further two were selected from outside the area to allow comparisons to be made. On average, 12 children from each school took part in the focus groups. Each group was presented with the same critical question: "What would you do to improve the area where you live?"

The focus groups worked extremely well and led to a wealth of suggestions and ideas from children about how their local areas could be improved. Over 40 responses, such as "stop selling and taking drugs" and "cut down pollution", were inputted into the computer software. These were randomly sorted into a series of questions, to test children's overall priorities. The questionnaire was then completed by 575 seven- to eleven-year-olds.

The top ten priorities were drawn from the children's questionnaires:

- stop drug-taking and drugs being sold;
- stop guns and knives being sold and used;

- stop strangers picking up children;
- give homeless people somewhere to live;
- take care of animals;
- stop people being robbed;
- put better police on the streets;
- look after old people better;
- stop racism;
- provide more for the disabled.

'DRUGS ARE SMALL, BUT THEIR EFFECTS ARE TALL'

In March 1997, a children's conference, titled 'What's your Problem? Listen to Children', was held at Liverpool Football Club's Anfield Stadium. The purpose of the conference was to celebrate and disseminate children's ideas for improving their local communities. The event affirmed children's enthusiasm and commitment, with over 80 children taking part from five schools. Children made presentations and performed poetry on a range of issues from drugs to community violence, to the dangers of smoking and the need for safe play areas. The children's positive regard for others was apparent, with repeated appeals for drug addicts to be treated with compassion and understanding.

At the end of the morning the children, who had earlier been wracked with nerves, asked the adult organisers: "Can we do it again this afternoon?" They were exhilarated and, having been through the dreaded performance once, were now ready to do it all over again.

Unfortunately, many of the adults who could have benefited from children's experiences and ideas that day had other priorities. Despite the best efforts of members of the Children's Research Group, only two adults with significant local power and influence attended – the chief executive of the city council and one local councillor. Mike Jones, who leads The Children's Society's work in the Liverpool 8 area, describes this event as 'seminal' in three main ways. First, it was an extremely positive experience for the children taking part. Second, it served to energise and strengthen the commitment of the Children's Research Group to promote children's active participation in community development and local regeneration initiatives. Less positively, it also highlighted that significant members of the local adult community were not sufficiently engaged with the need to listen to and learn from children.

As a first step to building bridges between children and adult decision-makers, a group of children who took part in the Anfield conference made a presentation to city councillors later that year. The children received a standing ovation, and the clerk to the council later commented that she had not witnessed such a positive response from councillors since a presentation from the families of those killed in the Hillsborough stadium tragedy.

CONDUCTING A FEASIBILITY STUDY

One of the recommendations from the Anfield conference was that a feasibility study should be carried out into a children's advocacy or rights bureau. There was increasing concern among a range of local organisations that children's and young people's effective long-term participation could only be achieved through co-ordinated action across all local agencies. Further, the need for a central mechanism to raise awareness, energise and facilitate the everyday practice of children's rights and participation was becoming more apparent.

In 1998, Save the Children, which had been running a child health project in the city, established a Children in Neighbourhoods group, whose members were drawn from the statutory, voluntary and community sectors. It was through this group that the idea of a bureau for children and young people started to become a reality. A reference group was formed in March 1999 of senior professionals from local health, police and education services. Representatives from voluntary organisations and academic bodies were also key members. Professor Ruth Hussey, director of public health for Liverpool Health Authority, chaired the group.

With joint funding from Liverpool City Council, Save the Children, The Children's Society and Liverpool's Council for Voluntary Service, a six-month feasibility study was launched in January 2000:

> To identify and assess the best ways in which to work in a
> sustainable way in partnership with the children and young people of

*Liverpool in order to achieve their greater participation and influence
in decisions and actions which affect their lives at local, regional,
national and international levels.*[2]

The first stage of the feasibility study was a conference attracting
almost 90 adult participants from a range of statutory, voluntary,
community and commercial organisations. The conference raised
many questions and concerns about how a bureau might operate,
particularly relating to whether children and young people should
lead it. There was repeated reference to the need for adult agencies to
demonstrate their commitment to children's rights practically. Three
major themes were raised by conference participants: the need for
independence; an emphasis on achieving positive change for and
with children; and the importance of working in partnership with
children and young people.

Priority areas for the Liverpool Bureau:

Taken from the search conference report (March 2000)

- Need for a follow-up event to present action plan and to have
  organisations and decision-makers pledge their commitment.
- Bureau needs to be independent.
- An audit should be carried out of existing services for children
  and young people that will prevent unnecessary duplication of
  work, and that will flag up important lessons of policy and
  practice that the Bureau can take forward.
- Need to ensure the work of the Bureau is taken seriously and
  opens up institutions to the challenge of real change.
- Need to consult a representative group of children and young
  people to ascertain their ideas and advice on the concept of a
  Liverpool Bureau.

Following the conference, a variety of methods were used to elicit
children's and adult's views and ideas. The National Opinion Poll
(NOP) organisation was commissioned to conduct two surveys with
children and parents; semi-structured interviews were carried out
with a range of local professionals and councillors; and focus groups
were used with children and adults from diverse backgrounds.
Additionally, members of the reference group visited several projects

carrying out innovative work across England. They also collected information about positive developments in children's rights and participation across the UK and further afield.

NINE OUT OF TEN CHILDREN SAID THEIR VIEWS WERE NEVER SOUGHT

The NOP asked 1,500 seven- to 18-year-olds a range of questions about their communities, and about children's rights and participation. Fewer than one in ten said they had ever been asked to express an opinion about their local community. Focus group discussions revealed that children and young people felt that councillors were more interested in parents' views than children's. Despite this, eight out of ten survey respondents thought that Liverpool was a good place for them to live. Primary school-aged children rated family and friends as most significant (26 per cent) while the most common response from secondary school-aged children was that there was a lot to do and see (24 per cent). Very few children and young people involved in the survey, or taking part in the focus groups, had any real understanding of the UNCRC.

Only one in three parents out of a sample of 500 said they had heard of the UNCRC. Focus groups and interviews with professionals showed that even when adults said they had heard about the UNCRC, further probing revealed widespread ignorance and misunderstanding.

BUREAU GETS THE THUMBS UP

There were many other factors that led the reference group to conclude that a bureau for children and young people is what Liverpool needs in order to further children's rights and participation. The feasibility study unearthed pockets of positive practice and progressive developments but these were not systematically promoted or shared across different settings or geographical areas. Often initiatives would be started, or children and young people consulted on a particular issue, but there was no follow-up action or external pressure to implement change. For example, a local councillor told the story of a young person attending a council meeting to make the case for a local facility for skateboarding. The councillor praised the young person:

> *It was encouraging to see young people come to the council... you need guts and you need to be a bit brave to stand up there in front of all the members of the council.*

Yet the young woman's efforts were in vain because nothing happened following the meeting. An independent bureau effectively supporting children and young people to influence decision-makers might have made all the difference in this case.

THE VISION

The goal for the Liverpool Bureau for Children and Young People was for it to be launched during 2001, with the following aims:

- To be an independent body with a structure and funding that ensures independence and stability.
- To operate in accordance with the principles and standards of the United Nations Convention on the Rights of the Child.
- To champion the fullest implementation of children's human rights.
- To benefit all children and young people up to the age of 18 years, with a particular emphasis on marginalised and socially excluded children.
- To lead in the establishment of effective and representative links with children and young people.

The Bureau will provide information, advice, support, consultancy and training, and will also undertake commissioned pieces of research and project work. It will not, however, provide individual advocacy to children and young people.

In addition to the Bureau for children and young people, the report from the feasibility study made three further recommendations:

- The establishment of a children's and young people's participation partnership, comprising representatives from key agencies and children and young people, to advise, support and guide the Bureau.

- A standing conference on children's and young people's participation to be held annually.
- The appointment of a children's champion to act as an ambassador for children's and young people's participation across Liverpool.[3]

There were three pressing strategic priorities for the Bureau prior to its launch. First, there was a need to attract core funding, and a mixture of statutory, voluntary and commercial support was sought. Second, children and young people needed to be consulted about their involvement in the Bureau, particularly in relation to its overall management and direction. Third, the Bureau needed some 'quick wins' in order to galvanise local support and develop its reputation among children, as well as adults. The issue of whether The Children's Society would have a continuing role once the Bureau was officially launched also needed to be resolved. Mike Jones, a major contributor to the whole process, said of this type of innovative development work:

> ... [It] is not a marathon. It's more a relay race and sometimes you need to pass on the baton.

PARTNERS IN CHANGE: WHAT'S IMPORTANT?

It is almost ten years since the first pilot survey was carried out with children in the Liverpool 8 area. The youngest children consulted then will now be approaching the official age of majority: nearly all of the 129 participants would have been eligible to vote in the 2001 general election.[4]

What lessons does this process have for organisations and local authorities that are similarly committed to children's rights and participation? Eight factors appear to have contributed to the successful completion of the feasibility study, and to the growing support and interest across Liverpool for a powerful regional catalyst and focal point for children's rights.

LONG-TERM VISION AND PERSEVERANCE

Key players involved in laying the foundation stones of the Bureau were members of the Children's Research Group back in 1993. They have remained in their respective organisations, and have enhanced their skills and expertise in supporting and working in partnership with local children and young people. Crucially, these key players have developed important links with adults sharing a similar commitment and vision for children's rights across different professional groupings and service areas.

STRATEGIC NETWORKING

Agencies have forged links with key decision-makers over the years, and they have secured the practical involvement of senior service providers to support cultural and organisational change.

PARTNERSHIP APPROACH

No single organisation has tried exclusively to own the concept of a bureau for children and young people. There is a longstanding history of statutory, voluntary and community organisations working together to effect change for children and families in the Liverpool 8 area. In other words, the rights and interests of children and young people have been put before organisational promotion or 'branding'.

SHARED VALUES AND FRAMEWORK

From the outset, this initiative has been unequivocally based on the principles and standards of the UNCRC. The thread of positive respect for children's inherent dignity and evolving capacities as human beings runs clearly throughout all activities.

GROUNDED IN CHILDREN'S AND YOUNG PEOPLE'S EXPERIENCE

The concept of a bureau for children and young people arose from research on children's concerns and perceptions of their local areas. The feasibility study's recommendation to establish a bureau has renewed effort to engage with and work in partnership with children and young people.

INVESTMENT IN LOCAL COMMUNITIES

Many of the individuals involved in this initiative over the past decade have lived or worked in Liverpool for many years. Organisations like The Children's Society have invested significant resources into the Liverpool 8 area, and have a longstanding commitment to the area.

ADULTS ARE THE PROBLEM, NOT THE CHILDREN

Those working with and consulting children and young people concluded early on that children's participation rights could only be realised if adults were helped to change. The challenge of children's and young people's participation has consistently been seen as resting with adults rather than being related to children's perceived misbehaviour or poor attitude.

OPENNESS AND FLEXIBILITY

Like so many participatory initiatives, the journey towards a bureau for children and young people in Liverpool has largely been uncharted territory. Key players have not allowed fear of the unknown to temper their hopes and dreams, and the whole process has been a lesson in openness and flexibility.

With hindsight, it is likely that the journey towards a bureau for children and young people could have happened more quickly. All the people holding onto, and developing, the vision for a children's and young people's bureau constantly had other pressing demands on their time and energy. The project would have benefited from a dedicated worker being employed to fuse the ambitions and hopes of all those involved into a strategic plan, with timescales and targets for fundraising.

It is also worth questioning whether children and young people could have been included as partners throughout the process, perhaps carrying out some of the research themselves. Their involvement in the development process would have required effective support, and it may have slowed down the process even further. However, it may also have resulted in a group of informed and skilled children and young people making decisions and influencing the Bureau from the earliest possible stages.

But the real story of Liverpool's Bureau for Children and Young People has only just begun. All the agencies that have been preparing for the start of the Bureau are committed to working in partnership with local children and young people. Thanks to the efforts and determination of a relatively small group of adults from a range of statutory and voluntary organisations across the 1990s, it is from this point forward that Liverpool's youngest citizens will take centre stage.

For more information about the Liverpool Bureau for Children and Young People, please contact:

Mike Jones
Children and Neighbourhoods in Liverpool Project
Upper Parliament Neighbourhood Centre
Crown Street
Liverpool
L8 7SA

Tel: 0151 709 8222
E-mail: citizens-now@childrenssociety.org.uk

CHAPTER 3

Seen, heard and taken seriously: what works in children's and young people's participation?

The 1990s saw The Children's Society and many other organisations pioneering new ways of listening to children and young people, and acting on their concerns and ideas.

The six case studies featured here represent only a selection of the organisation's work in children's and young people's participation. The projects were not selected because they were thought to be the 'best' examples of practice in this evolving area – they were chosen because they demonstrate a range of approaches. Both their successes and difficulties help to underline some key themes for positive practice in participatory work.

Several factors can be identified as being important to the success of participatory work in changing the culture and practice of organisations. These are:

- being clear about the purpose of participatory activities and events;
- acting *with*, rather than *for*, children and young people;
- tailoring methods to the needs and interests of children and young people;
- working within a rights and social justice framework;
- developing the experience and commitment of staff;
- ensuring resources match reality;
- promoting partnership working;
- encouraging reflection and development.

BEING CLEAR ABOUT THE PURPOSE OF PARTICIPATORY ACTIVITIES AND EVENTS

Not being clear or single-minded about the purpose of children's rights and participatory initiatives can lead to projects carrying out an enormous range of activities but ultimately not being able to produce concrete evidence of where decisions and policy and practice have positively changed as a result.

All of the six case studies reflect, to varying degrees, the focus and commitment needed to achieve positive change for, and with, children and young people. Too often children's and young people's participation is associated with adults simply listening, whereas the real point of participatory projects and approaches is to effect change. As Rachel Hodgkin and Peter Newell explain:

> *There seems a real danger these days that involving and listening to children will be seen by policy-makers and service-providers as an end in itself, rather than the means by which we work with children to get things changed for the better.*[1]

While it is crucial that those working directly with children to promote their rights and participation have change as their ultimate focus, organisations and institutions commissioning or benefiting from such initiatives also need to share this expectation.

ACTING *WITH* RATHER THAN *FOR* CHILDREN AND YOUNG PEOPLE

Working towards children's rights and participation is about helping children and young people to win respect and influence in decision-making processes. It follows, then, that participatory projects need to enable children and young people to have ownership of activities, as well as to shape priorities and agendas. This includes, wherever possible, being involved from the outset in planning projects, recruiting staff, carrying out aspects of the work and being involved in project monitoring and evaluation.

The six case studies offer some positive examples of children and young people as partners in the development and work of projects.

Early in its life, UCAN set up an advisory group to ensure local children and young people could influence its priorities and the direction of the project's work.

The concept for a Liverpool Bureau for Children and Young People arose from research with children and young people. When the idea was close to being realised, local children and young people were asked to shape its initial agenda and activities.

Young people were involved in the planning of both of the young carers' festivals, and took an active role in disseminating the messages from these innovative consultations.

Chris Martin and colleagues from the Speak Up, Speak Out group were very much in the driving seat of their disability equality work. Other young disabled people who took part in the Quality Protects multimedia consultation made their own choices about how to communicate their ideas and experiences, and selected the topics for discussion. Young disabled people were at the forefront of carrying out the research, deciding on the questions and venues for consultation sessions, as well as facilitating group and individual activities. They also actively promoted their work at national and local conferences.

Partnerships with children and young people help professionals keep on track, maintaining a sharp focus on the real needs and concerns of children and young people. For example, the UCAN advocacy project ensures systems work for children and young people, rather than the other way round. One of the project workers, a former social worker, reflected this emphasis:

My focus has changed completely. Then I had to have a general picture whereas now I am purely looking at the perspective of young people.

The Children's Society's national consultation for the Quality Protects programme gave children and young people the opportunity to reflect and advise on all areas of their lives, not just those associated with health or social care. The results strike a chord with many other consultations with children and young people, where young respondents consistently demand increased local leisure and play facilities. Yet leisure and play are not traditionally viewed as the concern of staff in health and social services.

Finally, the Genesis project works with school students but its activities are guided by children's and young people's whole needs, not simply those associated with education. One young person described the project as dealing with "all the things to do with out of school life".

METHODS TAILORED TO THE NEEDS AND INTERESTS OF CHILDREN AND YOUNG PEOPLE

Organisations need to tailor models and approaches to the particular needs of the children and young people they are working with, taking into account their ages, backgrounds and circumstances. The diversity of approaches reflected in the six case studies show the benefits of being flexible and open when supporting children and young people as partners in change.

For example, as part of the early years' project, consultations with very young children were carried out in settings familiar to them, and the project workers used a mixture of observation, play and discussion to elicit their views.

The disability equality work was initially carried out in a school as this avoided problems with arranging transport. It was hoped that running the group here would help the school develop its ethos and practice, as well as support individual young people to become more assertive and confident about expressing their views within this setting. Over time, the enormous benefits of using multimedia work were also realised.

The young carers' festivals were planned to provide a platform for children and young people to share their ideas and experiences, but project workers also had to ensure that the events were fun.

The Genesis project in schools shows how many different approaches, including one-to-one support and individual counselling, as well as group work and setting up school councils, can be used by the same project to help children and young people get the most from their school experience.

The UCAN advocacy project offers children and young people in care and those involved in child protection a different kind of professional support, where they are in charge of how their ideas and experiences are shared and used.

Finally, The Children's Society's work in Liverpool is founded on research on children's and young people's concerns, and knowledge of children's rights. The Liverpool Bureau for Children and Young People has an ambitious goal of achieving the social inclusion of local children and young people in all areas of life, and those involved know they must explore new methods of building bridges between children and young people and the adult community.

RIGHTS AND SOCIAL JUSTICE FRAMEWORK

Social justice for children and young people means valuing and regarding them as citizens of equal worth to adults. It recognises that children and young people face many challenges throughout their young lives, and that these difficulties are rooted in wider social and economic problems rather than being the fault of individual people, families or communities.

Working from a social justice framework means learning about, campaigning for and practically applying the UNCRC. This international treaty covers the breadth of childhood. It grants children and young people a range of participation rights but it also has implications for the provision of play and education, healthcare and social security, and support to those children and young people living in perilous conditions.

A commitment to children's human rights is invaluable in forging positive relationships and partnerships with children and young people. The reflections of children and young people involved in some of the six projects show how much they appreciate being respected and taken seriously as individuals. Of note are their observations that project staff are different from other professionals they know. For example, when Chris Martin reflected on The Children's Society's disability equality work, he referred repeatedly to the project leader's commitment to children's rights and to the empowerment of young disabled people.

While treating children and young people with respect and basic courtesy is not, of course, restricted solely to those adults who work from a social justice agenda, this framework nevertheless encourages such positive behaviour.

Importantly, a social justice framework also recognises the need to challenge negative images and perceptions of children and young people. Within British society there is still a tendency to underestimate children and young people and treat them as though they have much less than adults to contribute to decision-making – in the family, within educational settings, in local communities and in wider society. It is therefore not unusual for children and young people to internalise beliefs that they cannot take part in certain activities because of lack of skill or competency rather than because they have not had the opportunity or encouragement. This is a particular problem for young disabled people and for young children, whose contribution and capacities are frequently ignored or underestimated.

The Children's Society's work with young disabled people focuses on tackling their continuing social exclusion, but it has also necessarily involved supporting individual children and young people to reject and challenge disabling ideas and behaviour, so developing more positive views of themselves and their capacities.

The consultations with very young children as part of the early years project were premised on a belief that "children's feelings are as strong and valid as those of adults" and project workers were told to "earn children's trust by working with them as equals".

DEVELOPING THE EXPERIENCE AND COMMITMENT OF STAFF

While the commitment to listening to children and young people may have always been there, the last decade has brought a host of opportunities to learn, practice and experiment with working in a participatory way. Most organisations working with children and young people now have staff with experience of promoting participation in decision-making. Many have networked with others doing similar jobs locally, regionally, nationally and even internationally. This presents opportunities to share learning – for example, events, seminars, workshops and Internet discussion groups.

At The Children's Society, several 'programme managers' co-ordinate and develop particular areas of work, champion and support best practice, bringing project staff (and more recently young people) together to learn from each other, as well as regularly circulating information about policy and practice developments nationally and internationally.

RESOURCES TO MATCH REALITY

Effective participation can be extremely labour and time-intensive. Participatory work requires time to form relationships with children and young people, whether it is within the context of research, consultation, advocacy and community or wider political change. To work well together, children, young people and adults need to get to know and trust each other. This is particularly pertinent when considering the participation of young disabled people in decision-making, where they may communicate their views, wishes and ideas in non-verbal ways. Linda Ward, who has written widely on the subject of young disabled people's rights, attended the Ask Us! launch described earlier. After the presentations of children's and young people's multimedia work, she apologised for just using her voice to communicate, stating that:

This fabulous presentation shows all the other and better ways to be heard.

PARTNERSHIP WORKING

In different ways, all the case studies espouse the benefits of partnership working. The development of the Liverpool Bureau for Children and Young People is perhaps the biggest single example of collaborative working with organisations, both in the statutory and voluntary sectors. This should give the bureau a ready-made constituency, ensuring that key stakeholders are ready to listen to and work with its staff and children and young people.

The young carers' festivals would not have been possible without

The Children's Society forging links with the YMCA Fairthorne Manor, whose staff bring both their commitment to children's human rights and expertise in arranging large-scale activity events. The Genesis and UCAN projects show the value of voluntary organisations joining forces with statutory service-providers, offering children and young people different ways of getting their voices heard and acted upon within educational and social services settings.

The Children's Society disability equality work is an example of working with national partners, the Department of Health and the Joseph Rowntree Foundation. Here, staff and managers from The Children's Society saw a great opportunity for their work with young disabled people to be further developed and capitalised on at a national public policy level.

The case study on consulting very young children also affirms the importance of partnership working. One of the principal reasons for this three-year consultation project not achieving positive change for children was the lack of engagement from the commissioning organisations. This is a critical learning point that applies *within*, as well as *across*, organisations. Quite simply, participatory work will not achieve much if those holding power are not informed, connected and inspired to act.

REFLECTION AND DEVELOPMENT

Although most organisations now aspire to supporting children's and young people's effective participation, there is a constant pressure for early success and quick-wins.[2] However, adults need to be realistic about the timescales involved in participatory work with children and young people. The hours of preparation time needed to support a group of children and young people to speak confidently at a conference can easily be lost on an adult audience who see a well-rehearsed play or hear a poem being read with passion. The series of preparatory meetings and telephone conversations to ensure a child or young person feels equipped to speak in their child protection conference or school council is a hidden part of participatory work. That children and young people may have spent their evenings and weekends preparing for these events, and may have travelled long distances to take part, can also be lost on professionals. For example, the Ask Us! launch of six CDs, attended and run by young disabled people across the country, involved many setting off at the crack of dawn to arrive at the venue by midday, taking into account the need for regular journey breaks.

But not every event will go so smoothly. Children and young people may fail to turn up; they may forget their notes; their voices may be too quiet for a large meeting room; or they may be angry and argumentative. However, rather than relating this to a lack of experience or confidence of particular individuals, or to the environment not being conducive to participation, these instances can be used by sceptics to exclude children and young people further. It sometimes seems that higher expectations are held for young contributors to seminars, roundtable discussions, workshops or conferences than for adults. If a child or young person comes badly prepared, or arrives late, this is noted. Similar behaviour by adult participants is often less visible because there are so many of them and their behaviour is not scrutinised in the same way. This inevitably places pressure on staff who are supporting children and young people to express their ideas and views: there is a sense that events must go smoothly or the whole case for children's and young people's participation will be vulnerable to attack.

Project staff in each of the six case studies have a healthy acceptance that sometimes events or activities will not go as planned or desired, but that this is an inevitable part of working in new terrain. This requires confidence and experience, but it also helps if the wider organisation understands and supports learning and development, rather than criticises. Constructive evaluations of project work can support learning, as can annual reviews of staff development needs, and the successes and difficulties of achieving their objectives.

It is important to note that organisations that seek to support children and young people to effect change must also explore their own need for reform or, in some cases, radical transformation. They need to consider making serious moves to include children and young people at all levels of decision-making, including in the overall governance of the organisation, in staff selection and training, in publications and in designing and running projects. Such internal learning and capacity-building will undoubtedly enhance the confidence, skills and expertise of all those involved, thereby increasing their effectiveness in supporting other organisations to make space for children and young people.

CHAPTER

Now for the action...

WHAT YOU CAN DO TODAY TO PROMOTE CHILDREN'S AND YOUNG PEOPLE'S EFFECTIVE PARTICIPATION

These final points should help get the ball rolling, and speed up existing developments. In the end, though, a commitment to children's human rights and participation is a frame of mind and a way of living. It is not a nine-to-five occupation or a special project with targets to be met within certain timescales. It is about valuing babies, children and young people as fellow human beings and striving together for a better world where we can all live with respect and understanding. Be part of it.

Set aside half an hour to think about nothing else but your relationships with children and young people.

- How much do you support their right to contribute to decision-making?
- What practical examples come to mind where you have been instrumental in helping them express their views and be taken seriously?
- What would they say if asked whether you respect and value them as people?

Make a list of the potential opportunities within your organisation for children and young people to contribute to decision-making – in relation to them as individuals but also in policy and service development.

Now go through the list and consider where your organisation isn't making any progress, and where there is active engagement and positive action.

- Can you identify common themes? For example, is all the progress associated with one particular group of children or staff team?
- Has it been helpful to have the backing of senior people?
- What role has resources played?

Examine the messages staff in your organisation receive about the value and worth of children and young people.

- How are children and young people represented, for example, in your promotional materials and in job advertisements and job descriptions?
- What staff training opportunities are available on understanding and implementing children's human rights?
- How do new ideas and developments about children's and young people's participation filter through your organisation?
- Are negative attitudes challenged, and by whom?
- If a group of children and young people came to you today with a proposal for changing one aspect of your organisation's policy or practice, how long would it take for a final decision and the subsequent change to be made?

Think about the people in your organisation who can speed up or scupper progress.

- What makes some committed and others antagonistic?
- Whose involvement is crucial and who uses up unnecessary time and energy?

Try to recall an interesting project or innovation you read or heard about recently.

- Make contact with the people involved and ask them for more information on the essential ingredients for eliciting, and acting on, children's and young people's experiences and ideas.

Make a plan of action of what you can do from today to further promote children's and young people's participation rights.

- Mark your diary or calendar so that you take time out to go through these pages again at least once a month.

Further reading

RIGHTS AND PARTICIPATION – GENERAL

Arnstein, S. (1969) 'A Ladder of Citizen Participation in the USA', *Journal of the American Institute of Planners*, 35, 4, 216–24

Article 12 (1999) *RESPECT: A Report Into How Well Article 12 of the UN Convention on the Rights of the Child is Put into Practice Across the UK*

Baker, J. (1996) *The Fourth Partner: Participant or consumer?* Youth Work Press

Beresford, P. and Croft, S. (1993) *Citizen Involvement: A Practical Guide for Change*, Macmillan

Beresford, P. and Croft, S. (1993) *Getting Involved, A Practical Manual*, Open Services Project and Joseph Rowntree Foundation

Children's Rights Development Unit (1995) *Building Small Democracies: The Implications of the UN Convention on the Rights of the Child for Respecting Children's Civil Rights Within the Family*

Children's Rights Development Unit (1995) *Making the Convention Work for Children*

Dickenson, B. (2000) *The Youth of Today Have Something to Say... About Participation: The Story of the Participation Education Group*, Participation Education Group

Fajerman, L. *et al* (2000) *Children as Partners in Planning*, Save the Children

Flekkoy, M. G. and Kaufman, N. H. (1997) *The Participation Rights of the Child: Rights and Responsibilities in Family and Society*, Jessica Kingsley

Flekkoy, M. G. (1991) *A Voice for Children*, Jessica Kingsley Publishers

Franklin, R. (ed.) (1995) *The Handbook of Children's Rights*, Routledge

Hart, R. A. (1992) *Children's Participation: From Tokenism to Citizenship*, UNICEF Innocenti essays no. 4

Hodgkin, R. and Newell, P. UNICEF (1998) *Implementation Handbook for the UN Convention on the Rights of the Child*

John, M. (ed.) (1996) *Children in Charge: The Child's Rights to a Fair Hearing*, Jessica Kingsley Publishers

Lansdown, G. (2001) *Promoting Children's Participation in Democratic Decision-making*, UNICEF Innocenti Research Centre

Lansdown, G. (1995) *Taking Part: Children's Participation in Decision-making*, IPPR

Miller, J. (1999) *All Right at Home? Promoting Respect for the Human Rights of Children in Family Life*, Children's Rights Office

Nevison, C. (1996) *A Matter of Opinion: Research into Children and Young People's Participation Rights in the North East*, Youth Issues North, Save the Children

Save the Children (1999) *We Have Rights, Okay! Children's Views of the United Nations Convention on the Rights of the Child*

Save the Children (2001) *UN Convention on the Rights of the Child – An International Save the Children Alliance Training Kit*, CD-Rom.

Thames Valley Partnership (1997) *Speak Out: A Guide to Youth Consultation*

Thomas, N. (2000) *Children, Family and the State: Decision-making and Child Participation*, Macmillan

Tolley, E. *et al* (1998) *Young Opinions, Great Ideas*, National Children's Bureau

Treseder, P. (1995) *Empowering Children and Young People: Training Manual Promoting Involvement in Decision-making*, Save the Children and Children's Rights Office

Treseder, P. and Crowley, A. (2001) *Taking the Initiative: Promoting Young People's Participation in Decision-making: Wales Report*, Carnegie Young People Initiative

Wellard, S., Tearse, M. and West, A. (1997) *All Together Now: Community Participation for Children and Young People*, Save the Children

White, P. (2001) *Local and Vocal: Promoting Young People's Involvement in Local Decision-making. An overview and Planning Guide*, National Youth Agency

Willow, C. (1997) *Hear! Hear! Children and Young People's Democratic Participation in Local Government*, Local Government Information Unit

Willow, C. (1999) *It's Not Fair! Young People's Reflections on Children's Rights*, The Children's Society

Winter, M. (1997) *Children as Fellow Citizens: Participation and Commitment*, Radcliffe Medical Press

Youth Council for Northern Ireland (1993) *Participation, Youth Work Curriculum*

ADVOCACY

Children's Rights Officers and Advocates (1998) *On the Rights Track: Guidance for Local Authorities on Establishing Children's Rights and Advocacy Services*, Local Government Association

Dalrymple, J. and Hough, J. (1995) *Having a Voice: An Exploration of Children's Rights and Advocacy*, Venture Press

CENTRAL GOVERNMENT

Children and Young People's Unit (2001) *Learning to Listen: Core Principles for the Involvement of Children and Young People*

Children and Young People's Unit (2001) *Building a Strategy for Children and Young People*

Hodgkin, R. and Newell, P. (1996) *Effective Government Structures for Children*, Calouste Gulbenkian Foundation

Newell, P. (2000) *Taking Children Seriously: A Proposal for a Children's Rights Commissioner*, Calouste Gulbenkian Foundation

Office of the First Minister and Deputy First Minister (2001) *Protecting Our Children's Rights: A Consultation Paper on a Commissioner for Children for Northern Ireland*

CHILD PROTECTION

Cloke, C. and Davis, M. (1995) *Participation and Empowerment in Child Protection*, Pitman Publishing

Schofield, G. and Thoburn, J. (1996) *Child Protection: The Voice of the Child in Decision-making*, Institute for Public Policy Research

Thomas, N. and O'Kane, C. (1998) *Children and Decision-making: A Summary Report*, International Centre for Childhood Studies, University of Wales

CHILDREN AND YOUNG PEOPLE IN CARE

Children's Rights Officers and Advocates (2000) *Total Respect: Ensuring Children's Rights and Participation in Care*. Training pack produced for the Department of Health

Fletcher, B. (1993) *Not Just a Name: The Views of Young People in Foster and Residential Care*, National Consumer Council

Morris, S. and Wheatley, H. (1994) *Time to Listen: The Experiences of Children in Residential and Foster Care*, ChildLine

Wheal, A. and Sinclair, R. (1995) *It's YOUR Meeting: A Guide to Help Young People Get the Most from Their Review*, National Children's Bureau

Willow, C. (1996) *Children's Rights and Participation in Residential Care*, National Children's Bureau

CHILDREN IN NEIGHBOURHOODS

Adams, E. and Ingham, S. (1998) *Changing Places: Children's Participation in Environmental Planning*, The Children's Society

Fitzpatrick, S., Hastings, A. and Kintrea, K. (1998) *Including Young People in Urban Regeneration: A Lot to Learn*, Policy Press

Freeman, C. *et al* (1999) *Planning with Children for Better Communities*, The Policy Press

Hart, R. A. (1997) *Children's Participation: The Theory and Practice of Involving Young Citizens in Community Development and Environmental Care*, Earthscan

Henderson, P. (ed.) (1995) *Children and Communities*, Pluto Press

Kitchin, H. (2000) *Taking Part: Promoting Children and Young People's Participation for Safer Communities*, Local Government Information Unit

EDUCATION

Advisory Centre for Education (1995) *Children's Voices in School Matters*

Davies, L. and Fitzpatrick, G. (2000) *Euridem Project: A Review of Pupil Democracy in Europe*, Children's Rights Alliance for England

Garlake, T. and Pocock, M. (2000) *Partners in Rights: Creative Activities Exploring Rights and Citizenship for 7- to 11-year-olds*, Save the Children

Holden, C. and Clough, N. (ed.) (1998) *Children as Citizens: Education for Participation*, Jessica Kingsley

HEALTH

Children's Rights Development Unit (1995) *Child Health Rights: Implementing the UN Convention on the Rights of the Child*

Cohen, J. and Emanuel, J. (1998) *Positive Participation: Consulting and Involving Young People in Health-related Work: A Planning and Training Resource*, Health Education Authority

Department of Health (2000) *Make it Happen!*

Laws, S. (1998) *Hear Me! Consulting with Young People on Mental Health*, Mental Health Foundation

McNeish, D. (1999) *From Rhetoric to Reality: Participatory Approaches to Health Promotion with Young People*, Health Education Authority

RESEARCH AND ETHICS

Alderson, P. (1995) *Listening to Children: Children, Ethics and Social Research*, Barnardos

Kirby, P. (1999) *Involving Young Researchers: How to Enable Young People to Design and Conduct Research*, Joseph Rowntree Foundation

Save the Children (2000) *Young People as Researchers: A Learning Resource Pack*

YOUNG CHILDREN

Alderson, P. (2000) *Young Children's Rights: Exploring Beliefs, Principles and Practice*, Jessica Kingsley Publishers and Save the Children

Clark, A. and Moss, P. (2001) *Listening To Young Children: The Mosaic Approach*, National Children's Bureau

Kinney, L. and McCabe, J. (2000) *Children as Partners: A Guide to Consulting with Very Young Children and Empowering Them to Participate Effectively*, Stirling Council

Miller, J. (1999) *A Journey of Discovery: Children's Creative Participation in Planning*, Save the Children

Miller, J. (1996) *Never Too Young: How Children Can Take Responsibility and Make Decisions*, National Early Years Network and Save the Children

Save the Children (1996) *Children's Participation Pack: A Practical Guide for Playworkers*

Willow, C. and Hyder, T. (1999) *It Hurts You Inside: Children Talking About Smacking*, National Children's Bureau and Save the Children

YOUNG DISABLED PEOPLE

Ask Us! (2001), Summary CD for Quality Protects Consultation, The Children's Society

Jones, H. (2000) *Including Disabled People in Everyday Life: A Practical Approach*, Save the Children

Kirkbride, L. (1999) *I'll Go First: The Planning and Review Toolkit for Use with Children with Disabilities*, The Children's Society

Middleton, L. (1999) *Disabled Children: Challenging Social Exclusion*, Blackwell Science

Morris, J. (1995) *Gone Missing? A Research and Policy Review of Disabled Children Living Away from their Families*, Who Cares? Trust

Ward, L. (1997) *Seen and Heard: Involving Disabled Children and Young People in Research and Development Projects*, Joseph Rowntree Foundation

Useful contacts/Web addresses

Author:
Carolyne Willow
Children's Rights Alliance for England
319 City Road
London
EC1V 1LJ

020 7278 8222
E-mail: cwillow@primex.co.uk

Co-ordinator of Participation into Practice:
Bill Badham
Programme Manager
Children in Communities
The Children's Society
East Midlands Regional Office
Mayfair Court
Northgate
Nottingham
NG7 7GR

Tel: 0115 942 2974
E-mail: bill.badham@childrenssociety.org.uk

Genesis project/work with very young children:
Julie McLarnon or Simon Hepburn
91–93 Queens Road
Peckham
London
SE15 2EZ

Tel: 020 7639 1466
E-mail: julie.mclarnon@childrenssociety.org.uk
    simon.hepburn@childrenssociety.org.uk

UCAN project:
Janet Wyllie
UCAN
12 Hanbury Road
Pontypool
Torfaen
NP4 6JL

Tel: 01495 740744
E-mail: ucan@childrenssociety.org.uk

Young carers' festivals:
Jenny Frank
Young Carers Initiative
Youngs Yard
Finches Lane
Twyford
Nr Winchester
SO21 1NN

Tel: 01962 711511
E-mail: young-carers-initiative@childrenssociety.org.uk

Speak Up, Speak Out group:
Maureen Murray
St Christopher's Shared Care
625 Warwick Road
Solihull
B91 1AP

Tel: 0121 709 2610
E-mail: maureen.murray@childrenssociety.org.uk

Ask Us! national consultation:
Margaret Hart
8 Vine Street
Kersal
Salford
Manchester
M7 3PG

Tel: 0161 792 8885
E-mail: margaret.hart@childrenssociety.org.uk

Liverpool bureau for children and young people:
Mike Jones
Children and Neighbourhood Centre
Crown Street
Liverpool
L8 7AS

Tel: 0151 709 8222
E-mail: citizens-now@childrenssociety.org.uk

CHILDREN AND YOUNG PEOPLE'S WEBSITES

This selection of websites, based on a list from Sue Preston at the Warrington Project, has been expanded by The Children's Society Information & Library Service to include other sites. The sites mostly relate to children's activities, particularly play, welfare and rights. For convenience, they have been divided into sub-sections into: Play and creativity, Interactive, Children's rights, and General.

PLAY AND CREATIVITY

1 Fair Play for Children: www.arunet.co.uk/fairplay/
2 Kidsactive: www.kidsactive.org.uk
3 Centres for Curiosity and Imagination: www.centresforcuriosity.org.uk
4 National Playing Fields Association: www.npfa.co.uk
5 Action for Children's Arts: www.childrensarts.org.uk
6 Tocki 2000 (special needs equipment): www.tocki.co.uk
7 Letterbox Library: www.letterboxlibrary.com

INTERACTIVE

1 Pupiline: www.pupiline.net
2 Project Happy Child: www.happychild.org.uk
3 Gridclub: www.gridclub.com

CHILDREN'S RIGHTS

1 Article 12: www.article12.com
2 Playtrain (incorporating the Article 31 Network): www.playtrn.demon.co.uk
3 Children's Rights Alliance for England: www.crights.org.uk
4 Young Voice: www.young-voice.org.uk
5 Office of Children's Rights: Commissioner for London: www.londonchildrenscommissioner.org.uk

GENERAL

1   The Children's Society: www.childrenssociety.org
2   Department for Education and Skills: www.dfes.gov.uk
3   Childline: www.childline.co.uk
4   Trust for the Study of Adolescence: www.tsa.uk.com
5   Bullying Survival Guide:
    www.bbc.co.uk/education/archive/bully
6   Contact a Family: www.cafamily.org.uk
7   National Children's Bureau (NCB): www.ncb.org.uk
8   Young Minds: The Children's Mental Health Charity:
    www.youngminds.org.uk
9   Adders Organisation: (concerned with attention
    deficit/hyperactivity disorder): www.adders.org
10 BBC's Guide to Health and Fitness: www.bbc.co.uk
11 Sure Start: www.surestart.gov.uk
12 National Standards for Under-eights Daycare & Childminding:
    www.dfee.gov.uk/daycare
13 Child-friendly Initiative: www.childfriendly.org
14 Campaign for Learning: www.campaign-for-learning.org.uk
15 Childcare Link: www.childcarelink.gov.uk
16 Home Office: www.homeoffice.gov.uk
17 Children in Wales: www.childreninwales.org.uk
18 The Daycare Trust: www.daycaretrust.org.uk
19 Regard (Economic & Social Research Council):
    www.regard.ac.uk
20 Children's Legal Centre: www2.essex.ac.uk/clc/
21 Children and Young People's Unit: www.cypu.gov.uk
22 Save the Children: www.scfuk.org.uk

APPENDIX

United Nations Convention on the Rights of the Child

This is a summary of the main points of the UN Convention produced by UNICEF as *What Rights?*

ARTICLE 1

Everyone under 18 years of age has all the rights in this Convention.

ARTICLE 2

The Convention applies to everyone whatever their race, religion, abilities, whatever they think or say, whatever type of family they come from.

ARTICLE 3

All organisations concerned with children should work towards what is best for each child.

ARTICLE 4

Governments should make these rights available to children.

ARTICLE 5

Governments should respect the rights and responsibilities of families to direct and guide their children so that, as they grow, they learn to use their rights properly.

ARTICLE 6

All children have the right to life. Governments should ensure that children survive and develop healthily.

ARTICLE 7

All children have the right to a legally registered name, the right to a nationality and their right to know and, as far as possible, to be cared for by their parents.

ARTICLE 8

Governments should respect children's right to a name, a nationality and family ties.

ARTICLE 9

Children should not be separated from their parents unless it is for their own good, for example if a parent is mistreating or neglecting a child. Children whose parents have separated have the right to stay in contact with both parents, unless this might hurt the child.

ARTICLE 10

Families who live in different countries should be allowed to move between those countries so that parents and children can stay in contact or get back together as a family.

ARTICLE 11

Governments should take steps to stop children being taken out of their own country illegally.

ARTICLE 12

Children have the right to say what they think should happen, when adults are making decisions that affect them, and to have their opinions taken into account.

ARTICLE 13

Children have the right to get and to share information as long as the information is not damaging to them or to others.

ARTICLE 14

Children have the right to think and believe what they want and to practice their religion, as long as they are not stopping other people from enjoying their rights. Parents should guide their children on these matters.

ARTICLE 15

Children have the right to meet together and to join groups and organisations, as long as this does not stop other people from enjoying their rights.

ARTICLE 16

Children have a right to privacy. The law should protect them from attacks against their way of life, their good name, their families and their homes.

ARTICLE 17

Children have the right to reliable information from the mass media. Television, radio and newspapers should provide information that children can understand, and should not promote materials that could harm children.

ARTICLE 18

Both parents share responsibility for bringing up their children, and should always consider what is best for each child. Governments should help parents by providing services to support them, especially if both parents work.

ARTICLE 19

Governments should ensure that children are properly cared for, and protect them from violence, abuse and neglect by their parents or anyone else who looks after them.

ARTICLE 20

Children who cannot be looked after by their own family must be looked after properly, by people who respect their religion, culture and language.

ARTICLE 21

When children are adopted the first concern must be what is best for them. The same rules should apply whether the children are adopted in the country where they were born or taken to live in another country.

ARTICLE 22

Children who come into a country as refugees should have the same rights as children born in that country.

ARTICLE 23

Children who have any kind of disability should have special care and support so that they can lead full and independent lives.

ARTICLE 24

Children have the right to good quality health care and to clean water, nutritious food and a clean environment so that they will stay healthy. Rich countries should help poorer countries achieve this.

ARTICLE 25

Children who are looked after by their local authority rather than their parents should have their situation reviewed regularly.

ARTICLE 26

The Government should provide extra money for the children of families in need.

ARTICLE 27

Children have a right to a standard of living that is good enough to meet their physical and mental needs. The Government should help families who cannot afford to provide this.

ARTICLE 28

Children have a right to an education. Discipline in schools should respect children's human dignity. Primary education should be free. Wealthy countries should help poorer countries achieve this.

ARTICLE 29

Education should develop each child's personality and talents to the full. It should encourage children to respect their parents, and their own and other cultures.

ARTICLE 30

Children have a right to learn and use the language and customs of their families, whether these are shard by the majority of people in the country or not.

ARTICLE 31

All children have a right to relax and play, and to join in a wide range of activities.

ARTICLE 32

The Government should protect children from work that is dangerous or might harm their health or their education.

ARTICLE 33

The Government should provide ways of protecting children from dangerous drugs.

ARTICLE 34

The Government should protect children from sexual abuse.

ARTICLE 35

The Government should make sure that children are not abducted or sold.

ARTICLE 36

Children should be protected from any activities that could harm their development.

ARTICLE 37

Children who break the law should not be treated cruelly. They should not be put in prison with adults and should be able to keep in contact with their families.

ARTICLE 38

Governments should not allow children under 15 to join the army. Children in war zones should receive special protection.

ARTICLE 39

Children who have been neglected or abused should receive special help to restore their self respect.

ARTICLE 40

Children who are accused of breaking the law should receive legal help. Prison sentences for children should only be used for the most serious offences.

ARTICLE 41

If the laws of a particular country protect children better than the articles of the Convention, then those laws should stay.

ARTICLE 42

The Government should make the Convention known to all parents and children.

The Convention on the rights of the child has 54 articles in all. Articles 43–54 are about how adults and governments should work together to make sure all children get all their rights.

A convention is an agreement between countries to obey the same law. When the government of a country ratifies a convention, that means it agrees to obey the law written down in that convention.

The United Kingdom of Great Britain and Northern Ireland ratified the Convention on the Rights of the Child on 16 December 1991. That means our government now has to make sure that every child has all the rights in the Convention.

Notes

INTRODUCTION

1 Page, R. and Clark, G. A. (ed.) (1977) *Who Cares?*, National Children's Bureau, page 62.

2 Children and Young People's Unit (November 2001) *Learning to Listen: Core Principles for the Involvement of Children and Young People*.

3 Hart, R. A. (1992) *Children's Participation: From Tokenism to Citizenship*. UNICEF, page 5.

4 Cutler, D. and Frost, R. (2001) *Taking the Initiative: Promoting Young People's Involvement in Public Decision-making in the UK*, Carnegie Young People Initiative, page 6.

CHAPTER 1: POLICY CONTEXT FOR CHILDREN'S AND YOUNG PEOPLE'S PARTICIPATION

1 The Unit's plans to promote children's and young people's effective partnership are described in *Tomorrow's Future. Building a Strategy for Children and Young People* (March 2001).

2 The UK ratified the UN Convention on the Rights of the Child on 16 December 1991.

3 The two countries that have not yet ratified the Convention are Somalia and the United States.

4 See, for example, the Universal Declaration of Human Rights and the European Convention on Human Rights, both of which apply to children and adults.

5 The Government's second report to the Committee on the Rights of the Child was published in August 1999. It gives little attention to progress on children's participation rights, even though these are central to the Convention. Conversely, each of the following reports prepared by non-governmental organisations examine in details children's participation in decision-making in a range of settings:

- Willow, C. (1999) *It's Not Fair! Young People's Reflections on Children's Rights*, The Children's Society.
- Fisher, A. *et al* (1999) *RESPECT! A Report Into How Well Article 12 of the UN Convention on the Rights of the Child is Put Into Practice Across the UK*, Article 12.
- Save the Children (1999) *We Have Rights, Okay! Children's Views of the United Nations Convention on the Rights of the Child*, Save the Children.

6 The UK Government's progress on fully implementing the Convention on the Rights of the Child should have been considered by the Committee on the Rights of the Child in 1999. However, the Committee has a serious backlog of reports, due to the almost universal ratification of this international treaty.

7 The Children's Rights Alliance for England (CRAE) has a public register of organisations in England that have formally adopted the Convention.

8 Willow, C. in Utting, D. (ed.) (1998) *Children's Services Now and In the Future*, National Children's Bureau.

9 *Young Prisoners: A Thematic Review by HM Chief Inspector of Prisons for England and Wales.* (November 1997), HMSO

10 Sections 48 and 49 of the Criminal Justice and Police Act 2001 grant local authorities and the police the power to introduce child curfew schemes for under-16-year-olds.

11 See Children's Rights Office (1995) *Building Small Democracies: The Implications of the UN Convention on the Rights of the Child for Respecting Children's Civil Rights Within the Family.*

12 See McCausland, J. (2000) *Guarding Children's Interests: The Contribution of Guardians Ad Litem to Court Proceedings*, The Children's Society.

13 See Hodgkin, R. and Newell, P. (1998) *Implementation Handbook for the Convention on the Rights of the Child*, UNICEF, pages 75–83.

14 Children's Rights Office (1995) *Building Small Democracies: The Implications of the UN Convention on the Rights of the Child for Respecting Children's Civil Rights Within the Family*, page 14.

15 Free nursery school places have been available since the end of 1997 for every four-year-old whose parents want them. The Government has further pledged that free education places will be available for 66 per cent of three-year-olds by 2001–2002.

16 DFES (November 2001) *Special Educational Needs Code of Practice*, page 29.

17 Department for Education and Employment (2000) *Education of Young People in Care: Guidance.*

18 OFSTED (September 2001) *Improving Inspection, Improving Schools.*

19 Article 29 of the UN Convention on the Rights of the Child states that the aims of education should include, "the development of the child's personality, talents and mental and physical abilities to their fullest potential".

20 The Act has been criticised for the way it allows schools and local education authorities to continue segregating young disabled people in 'special schools' if inclusion is "incompatible with the wishes of parents, or the provision of efficient education for other children".

21 Section 59 of the Children Act 1975 stated, "in reaching any decision relating to a child in their care, a local authority shall... so far as is reasonably practicable, ascertain the wishes and feelings of the child regarding the decision and give due weight according to his age and understanding".

22 Social care standards relating to: leaving care services (1996); foster care (1999); adoption (2001) and independent advocacy (2001 – draft) all stress the right of children and young people to be consulted and involved in decision-making.

23 Department of Health SSI (1998) *Someone Else's Children: Inspections of Planning and Decision-making for Children Looked After and the Safety of Children Looked After.*

24 Taken from the Department of Health Local Authority Circular 22 (2000) 13 November 2000.

25 See Bigg, T. (1997) *Report on Earth Summit II: the UN General Assembly Special Session to Review Outcomes from the Rio Summit,* UNED–UK.

26 See Adams, E. and Ingham, S. (1998) *Changing Places: Children's Participation in Environmental Planning,* The Children's Society.

27 The Community Foundation Network administers the Local Fund Network, worth £70 million over three years.

28 National Assembly for Wales (April 2000) *Communities First: Regenerating Our Most Disadvantaged Communities – a Consultation Paper.*

29 DETR (June 1998) *Modern Local Government: In Touch With the People.*

30 DETR (2000) *Best Value Performance Indicators for 2001/2002.*

31 Department of Health and Department for Education and Employment (1996) *Children's Services Planning: Guidance.*

32 National Assembly for Wales (November 2000) *Children and Young People: A Framework for Partnership: Consultation Document.*

33 Department for Education and Employment (1999) *Early Years Development and Childcare Partnerships: Planning Guidance 2000–2001.*

34 See Connexions Service National Unit (July 2001) *The Active Involvement of Young People in the Connexions Service. A Practitioners Guide.*
Connexions Service National Unit (July 2001) *The Active Involvement of Young People in the Connexions Service. A Managers Guide.*

35 Children's Rights Officers and Advocates (2000) *TOTAL RESPECT: Ensuring Children's Rights and Participation in Care.*

36 Kitchin, H. (2000) *Taking Part. Promoting Children and Young People's Participation for Safer Communities,* LGIU

37 See Children's Rights Alliance for England (2000) *The REAL Democratic Deficit: Why 16- and 17-year-olds Should be Allowed to Vote.*

38 Following the June 2001 general election, John Denham MP was appointed as the new Minister for Children and Young People.

39 Children and Young People's Unit (2001) *Learning to Listen: Core Principles for the Involvement of Children and Young People* and *Building a Strategy for Children and Young People.*

40 The Children's National Service Framework was announced in February 2001. It will cover all health and social care services to children and young people, including maternity and social services, and child and adolescent mental health services.

41 See Foreign and Commonwealth office (July 2000) *Children's Select Committee: Report on Children's Rights. Response of Her Majesty's Government.*

42 See *ChildRIGHT* 176 (May 2001) for a summary of the UK Youth Parliament's Youth Manifesto.

43 The United Nations General Assembly Special Session on Children (UNGASS) was originally scheduled for 19–21 September 2001 but was postponed due to the terrorist bombings in New York and Washington.

44 National Assembly for Wales (July 2001) *Moving Forward: Listening to Children and Young People in Wales: Proposal for Consultation.*

45 Dickenson, B. (1999) *The Youth of Today Have Something to Say... About Participation*, Participation Education Group.

46 See 'The teenagers who cannot vote', *The Guardian*, 6 June 2001.

CHAPTER 2: CHILDREN'S HUMAN RIGHTS AND SOCIAL INCLUSION

1 Alderson, P. (2000) *Young Children's Rights: Exploring Beliefs, Principles and Practice*, Jessica Kingsley.

2 Willow, C. (1999) *It's Not Fair! Young People's Reflections on Children's Rights*, The Children's Society.

3 Tim Davies, one of the young steering group members for this project, provided these useful insights.

4 See Voice for the Child in Care (1998) *Sometimes You've Got to SHOUT TO BE HEARD: Stories From Young People in Care About Getting Heard and Using Advocates.*

5 See Hodgkin, R. and Newell, P. (1996) *Effective Government Structures for Children: Report of a Gulbenkian Foundation Inquiry*, Calouste Gulbenkian Foundation.

6 Flekkoy, M. G. and Kaufman, N. H. (1997) *Rights and Responsibilities in Family and Society*, Jessica Kingsley Publishers, page 139.

7 See Lansdown, G. (1995) *Taking Part: Children's Participation in Decision-making*, Institute for Public Policy Research, and Willow, C. (1996) *Children's Rights and Participation in Residential Care*, National Children's Bureau.

8 Newell, P. in Henderson, P. (ed.) (1995) *Children and Communities*, Pluto Press.

9 Alderson, P. (2000) *Young Children's Rights: Exploring Beliefs, Principles and Practice*, Jessica Kingsley, page 64.

10 See Aries, P. (1962) *Centuries of Childhood*, Jonathan Cape, and Pinchbeck, I. and Hewitt, M. (1973) *Children in English Society*, Routledge and Kegan Paul.

11 Hillman, M. *et al* (1990) *One False Move: A Study of Children's Independent Mobility*, Policy Studies Institute.

12 Franklin, R. (ed.) (1995) *The Handbook of Children's Rights*, Routledge, page 11.

13 Utting, W. (1997) *People Like Us: The Report of the Review of the Safeguards for Children Living Away From Home*, The Stationery Office, page 109.

14 Waterhouse, R. (2000) *Lost in Care – Report of the Tribunal of Inquiry Into the Abuse of Children in Care in the Former County Council Areas of Gwynedd and Clwyd Since 1974*, Paras 29.49 and 29.50.

15 See Miller, J. (1999) *All Right at Home? Promoting Respect for the Human Rights of Children in Family Life*, Children's Rights Office.

16 This paragraph is based on personal communication from Tim Davies, one of the project's young steering group members.

17 The Children's Society (2001) *Young People's Charter of Participation.*

18 National Youth Agency and Local Government Association (2001) *Hear by Right*

19 Arnstein, S. (1969) A ladder of citizen participation in the USA, *Journal of the American Institute of Planners*, 35, 4, 216–24

20 Hart, R. A. (1992) *Children's Participation: From Tokenism to Citizenship*, Innocenti Essay No. 4, UNICEF, Innocenti Research Centre, Florence.

21 Hart, R. A. (1997) *Children's Participation: The Theory and Practice of Involving Young Citizens in Community Development and Environmental Care*, Earthscan, London.

22 Willow, C. (1999) *It's Not Fair! Young People's Reflections on Children's Rights*, The Children's Society, page 39.

23 Durrant, J. (1999) *The Status of Swedish Children and Youth Since the Passage of the 1979 Corporal Punishment Ban*, Save the Children.

24 Alderson, P. (1993) *Children's Consent to Surgery*, Open University Press, page 31.

25 Utting, D. (ed.) (1998) *Children's Services Now and in the Future*, National Children's Bureau.

26 Newell, P. in Henderson, P. (ed.) (1995) *Children and Communities*, Pluto Press, page 198.

CASE STUDIES

RESPECTING THE WHOLE CHILD: THE GENESIS SCHOOL INCLUSION PROJECT

1 All quotations, unless otherwise stated, are from young people who met the author to describe and reflect on the work of the project.

2 Not all computers are accessible to children and young people due to the need to protect confidential information.

3 *Schools: Building on Success*, Green paper, S Department for Education and Employment, 2001

CHANGING THE CHILD PROTECTION SYSTEM: THE UCAN ADVOCACY PROJECT

1 All quotes, unless otherwise stated, are from young people who met the author to describe and reflect on the work of the project.

2 Quotation from Jan Wyllie, project leader.

3 Utting, W. (1997) *People Like Us: The Report of the Review of Safeguards for Children Living Away from Home*, The Stationery Office, page 111.

4 Hansard House of Lords 13 January 2000 Vol. 608 No. 22, Columns 804–5.

5 Waterhouse, R. (2000) *Lost in Care – Report of the Tribunal of Inquiry into the Abuse of Children in Care in the Former County Council Areas of Gwynedd and Clwyd Since 1974*, The Stationery Office.

6 Department of Health *et al* (1999) *Working Together to Safeguard Children*.

7 UCAN advocacy for children and young people, *Annual Report April 2000–March 2001*, page 12.

8 The Children's Society (1999) *The Last Rung of the Ladder: An Examination of the Use of Advocacy by Children and Young People in Advancing Participation Rights in Practice Within the Child Protection System*.

9 Children's Rights Officers and Advocates (2000) *TOTAL RESPECT: Ensuring Children's Rights and Participation in Care*.

RESEARCH IN A FIELD: THE YOUNG CARERS' FESTIVALS

1 ONS (1996) *Young Carers and Their Families*.

2 Frank, J. (1999), *Couldn't Care More*, The Children's Society.

3 Saul Becker founded the Young Carers Research Group at Loughborough University in 1992. Early publications include Aldridge, J. and Becker, S. (1993) *Children Who Care: Inside the World of Young Carers* and Dearden, C. and Becker, S. (1995) *Young Carers – the Facts*.

4 Meridian Broadcasting Charitable Trust (1998) *Talking About It: Promoting Mental Health in Schools, an Education Resource*.

5 Frank, J., Tatum, C. and Tucker, S. (1999) *On Small Shoulders: Learning from the Experiences of Former Young Carers*, The Children's Society.

6 Frank, J., Tatum, C. and Tucker, S., Op. Cit., page 25.

7 Ibid, page 11.

8 Unless otherwise stated, all quotations in this section are taken from the festival magazine: *Young Carers Festival Voice: Review of the Young Carers' Festival 2000*, YMCA Fairthorne Manor and The Children's Society.

9 Priority Search® is a computer research programme that enables the priorities of initial participants to shape research questions.

ASK US! YOUNG DISABLED PEOPLE GET ACTIVE

1 All quotes, unless otherwise stated, are from direct communication with Chris Martin.
2 Ask Us! summary CD (2001) The Children's Society.
3 Author notes from Ask Us! launch conference.

SMALL VOICES COUNT TOO: THE CHILDREN'S SOCIETY UNDER-EIGHTS DEVELOPMENT PROJECT

1 One of the outcomes of the project has been for The Children's Society to develop a position statement on "What The Children's Society believes about listening to very young children".
2 *London on Your Doorstep* (2001), Save the Children and The Children's Society

CITIZENS NOW: THE LIVERPOOL BUREAU FOR CHILDREN AND YOUNG PEOPLE

1 Toxteth and Liverpool 8 are terms used to describe a similar geographic area – for the purpose of this case study the term Liverpool 8 has been used.
2 *Citizens Now! A Report into Children's Participation in Liverpool; Does the City Need a Children's Bureau?* Liverpool Council for Voluntary Services, Save the Children and The Children's Society, page 8.
3 Similar initiatives have been established by Save the Children in Oxfordshire and by the Children's Rights Alliance for England in London.
4 Liverpool 8 is part of the Riverside constituency, which had the lowest turnout in the 1997 and 2001 general elections, at 51.9 per cent and 34 per cent respectively of the electorate voting.

CHAPTER 3: SEEN, HEARD AND TAKEN SERIOUSLY: WHAT WORKS IN CHILDREN'S AND YOUNG PEOPLE'S PARTICIPATION?

1 Hodgkin, R. and Newell, P. (ed.) (2001) *UK Review of Effective Government Structures for Children 2001. A Gulbenkian Foundation Report*, page 28
2 This, of course, is also important for children and young people who can become demoralised by not having concrete examples of where their contribution is having an impact.